Richard Todd Canton

Cats & Dogs are People Too!

This Way is My Way

iUniverse, Inc.
Bloomington

Cats & Dogs are People Too!
This Way is My Way

iUniverse books may be ordered through booksellers or by contacting:

iUniverse
1663 Liberty Drive
Bloomington, IN 47403
www.iuniverse.com
1-800-Authors (1-800-288-4677)

ISBN: 978-1-4620-3219-8 (sc)
ISBN: 978-1-4620-2572-5 (ebook)

Printed in the United States of America

iUniverse rev. date: 6/3/2011

Cats & Dogs are People Too!

Hello there, come on in and welcome to the comfort of my home. Please say hello to my wife Sherry and to our house-pets. Within the pages of this book you will catch a glimpse into the lives of our family that exists on the inside of the four walls of our home.

Since we have no kids of our own, people often assume that our pets have become our children. Well, I think it runs a little deeper than that. It has to do with how much love is exchanged between man and beast. That love can run pretty deep where certain individuals are concerned. I may very well be one of those.

In telling my stories you will see just how much love one man can carry in his heart for those he loves. These stories are inspired by some animals from my past that have left a significant impression on me. Samantha, Chum, Daisy, Amy, Blinky, Nipper, Mr Stub, Flip, Ralph, Duke & Duchess and Poochie, just to name a few. Let me introduce you to our family and you can decide for yourself.

As a boy I found pets to be taken for granted. Our family had Sam the cat who had kittens every year. That was a time when you did not pay a vet to have your pet spayed or neutered, so it happened year after year. Dad decided to handle the situation by taking Sam a good stretch outside of town and drop her off, near the dump I think, and guess what? After a summer of rummaging thru life, she found her way home. Chum was a pet of ours that spent his life tied outdoors in our backyard, barking. Had I known then what I know now I would have done things differently. I realize now that his barking was brought about by keeping him on a short

1

leash. Looking back I see now that all he ever wanted was to be one of us, laughing and playing.

Luckily, he found a home on a farm over the border in New Brunswick but if I had it to do all over again, I would make it up to you boy. I would play fetch, chase you around, run beside you and get to know you for the beautiful canine that you were. Chum, you would be happy to know that today, I appreciate all animals that I come in contact with and that I have a great appreciation for all living things and that boy, is because of you. God Bless You and keep you until one day you and I can meet again and I prove myself to be a better human because of you.

It all Starts with Rory

Rory is Maine Coon Cat who have given a new meaning to what a gentleman is and respect for the colour orange.

I have to start out by saying, I never wanted a cat. It's not that I didn't like them or anything like that, I just didn't want the responsibility.

Becoming pet owners started out the same way for us as it does for a lot of folks. We took in a pet from a family member who could no longer properly care for it. That's how Rory the cat came to live with us. He was already full grown and despite his pretty orange exterior and fluffy coat, he was a determined and wilful cat. Rory did not want to be an indoor pet. He also did not want to be neutered and he did not want to be anybody's fuzzy wuzzy cuddly baby. He was determined to be free and tried nearly every type of escape known to man (and cat) quite often getting on my sorry nerves.

Over time he did learn to adjust to this quiet and comfortable lifestyle, but every once in a while he would sit in the downstairs window and let out a mournful howl, usually at four in the morning. I believe this was a result of his long lost freedom that Mommy and myself had robbed him of and his way of letting us know it..

To keep Rory from dying of boredom we purchased a kitten from a pet store. We did this in hopes that he could have a compatible playmate. Compared to Rory, who by this time was becoming a massive lion, this little black kitten (whom I named India) was just a little sprig. Feisty from her days in the cat orphanage she stood right up to Rory and warned him off with a few hisses. With that he dropped ever so gently onto his back and thrust forward his right paw in offering friendship and trust. It was at that moment that he was declared "the Gentle Giant". His actions seem to say to her "there are no enemies here".

India gave him a good going over and soon the two of them were inseparable. They would nap together on the rocking chair or curled up together on the cat bed on the trunk in the hall. The two of them were content with each other's company and so onward went our clean, quiet and indoor life.

I believe that everything I ever learned about comfort I learned from a cat. Each one of or pampered pets have enjoyed the luxury of their own personal sunbeams and favourite lounging areas. Slumber is a big part of this existence and one might only lift their groggy head long enough to give Daddy a goodbye glance as he left home for work. Rory and India had a glorious two years together until Daddy did the unthinkable; he brought home another half-grown kitten.

India was furious not just at me but at Rory and the new cat, Angel. She dissolved any feelings she had for Rory and found comfort at the foot of Daddy and Mommy's bed. She has resided there ever since. Rory, as with India, was a welcoming force to this street-wise and energetic tigress. The two of them bonded right away and a great comrade was formed between them. Why he took to these strangers was something I could never quite figure out but it was satisfactory to him that they came into what was once his sole home and was now a shelter for cats and kittens alike.

Angel took the opportunity to ingratiate herself into his life and did her best to keep him in line. Quite often she would put the run to him if he were bothering her or might give him a big bath if that's what she felt he needed at the time. Whatever it was, this little vixen, at half the size of Rory was totally in charge of him and that's just the way he liked it.

What I didn't know at the time of Angel's arrival was that she was sick with feline-leukaemia, a deadly and contagious disease. It ultimately took her life. The disease should have been passed onto Rory as he and Angel were so close but it was India who picked up the virus. I was shocked and saddened by both the death of Angel and the repercussions that this disease left behind. Confused as to what to do next I did the necessary research to see if there was indeed anything we could do to prolong India's life. I was, to say the least, unsure of her fate.

So, have you heard enough? I wanted to find a way to present Rory to you so that you could understand the gentleman that he really is and what a valuable part of this household he has become. At fourteen years of age he is more handsome and regal than ever and we couldn't be happier. He also photographs very well. He has been diagnosed with diabetes and requires daily shots of insulin. We have been both praised and criticized for the decision to prolong his life as it can be expensive but hey, what are we if not responsible pet owners?

That is exactly who we are. Despite many trips to the vet to regulate him and with all the prodding and poking that boy has had to endure, he has proven to one and all that he is a resilient and patient soul and is able to take whatever we dish out. The last time he went to the vet for a day visit he was so ragged looking that it broke my heart. As the vet's assistant took him into the room for yet another sample I could see the weariness in his eyes. No biting or scratching here, just compliance. At home Mommy tests his blood with the gluco-meter and Rory sits ever so cooperatively on her lap purring, while she does her work. Afterward he goes about his routine as casual as can be. All who know him have come to love him and I am no exception. Now that he seems to be regulated and is noticeably feeling better I can safely say how happy that makes Mommy and me.

India von halkien

I was never a cat lover. I adored kittens but I never felt that I would ever own one or ever form an attachment to one. That is until I met a little black kitten with green eyes. She was odd and determined and I was able to see something in her that peaked my interest. This little vixen formed an attachment to me and me to her. I was flattered by her devotion, amused by her determination, and astonished by her unique personality.

Unusual cat with an unusual name. I chose the name India von halkien from a character on the soap the Guiding Light. This little kitten grew into an exotic beauty but to tell the truth I sometimes forget that she is grown. I guess that I will always see her as my baby.

My family questions my sanity. They do know that I have a great love for the animal kingdom and they also know that someday I hope to visit the wild plains of Africa, but they also think the attraction between India and me is unnatural. She was the runt of the litter she was born in and sold to, a pet store for profit. I purchased her but strongly feel that I was the one who profited. Her devotion to me has made me stop and take a look at my life and to evaluate it's true worth. What exactly is important, where am I going, and what the hell do I hope to achieve.

Well, this is the way I see it. If you have love in your life then all else will fall into place. On the days that my phone doesn't ring and no one knocks on my door, I may find myself alone but I am not lonely. I am greeted at the door every day. I never eat or sleep alone and I absolutely never sit and watch television without my constant companion. She will wake from the deepest sleep when I come home just to be near me. She sits patiently while I have a shower and then follows me to whatever room I go into next and sit with me while I relax.

It is no wonder older folks find such comfort in animals. That, along with the fact that their families have all but abandoned them and one other reason that a lot of people don't realize. When a person reaches a certain age they are able to realize just how close to GOD they have come and in doing so reach for HIS highly prized possessions for comfort, and they for him.

India despises the other house-cats that reside in our home. If she feels any one of them is moving in her territory she will quickly put the run to them. She has a massive temper and is not afraid to fight to the death for her Daddy if she has to. Her appetite is the same as mine and she loves to sample anything that I am eating. So much so that I often have to lock her up for the duration of a meal so my wife and I can have a little peace and quiet.

Speaking of quiet, if I should accidentally lock her out of a room, she lets me no in no uncertain terms that she is not pleased. She is able to let out a desperate howl which can be heard all over our house. The mournful tone it takes on makes me feel like a bad parent (I mean owner!). The vet says she's one of the most hateful and uncooperative clients she has ever come across. Perhaps it's the hissing and growling or maybe even the deadly swipes she takes at all who come in contact with, or even the overwhelming dramatics involved with our yearly vet visits. Whatever it is, she makes her point known. India von halkien does what she wants to do when she wants to do it! She might even play with the other cats in our house but I warn you, it has to be on her terms or guess what? Game over.

Her teeth are gorgeous and coat is shiny. Overall her health is great despite the fact that she was diagnosed with feline-leukemia when she was three years old, she recently turned fourteen. Who knows how long she will live? I certainly don't.

My wife Sherry says that she believes that I have given her the will to live and that's why she's stuck around for so long. On those

7

evenings that I work late, my wife tells me she starts pacing around 9PM anxious for her Daddy to get home. I get a night lunch, turn on the TV in the bedroom and crawl in. My wife, by this time usually has drifted off so I try to be quiet. India makes herself comfortable anywhere on our bed and (usually leaning up against me) proceeds to have a bath. She too drifts off to sleep sometimes so comfortably that she begins to snore. I nudge her gently to snap her out of it but before long she's back to dreamland.

I urge all my friends to have their pets spayed and neutered and to keep them indoors. I preach this to all I meet. Since we follow this pattern it is easy to see that our pets flourish. That ladies and gentlemen is a good thing!

Another Boy

I have never been able to pass by an abandoned or neglected animal or look the other way where they are concerned. So I brought into our clutch an abandoned tiger striped cat that brought to our lives, a feisty and strong willed personality, strength and resilience and unfortunately feline-leukaemia. Despite the bleak news our Angel is someone who has made a significant impression on me.

When Angel passed away, something in me came alive. I guess it was awareness of just how fragile life is and how very temporary. If it was not for memories we really would have nothing to reflect upon and in a way that might have been a good thing. On the other hand I guess we would continue to make the same mistakes over and over without ever learning how to avoid such a thing.

A young woman who worked for me was anticipating becoming a cat owner. It seems this nice lady who lived out in the country, had many cats and she was going to supply the kitten. When she brought the two tone kitten into see us, the young woman decided that she had better not take it home with her, so I did.

My wife had still suffered in her grief over Angel and was not ready to accept another pet. She insisted that Rory and India were enough. Still, the little beige and white kitten with a little goatee eventually won her over. He too joined our family. I named him Robbie after my best friend. It was either that or Tim Horton, I think I made the right choice.

As this boy grew he became more and more skittish and nervous. This was something I found difficult to relate to. What on earth would he have to be scared of? All of them are indoor pets so whatever it was that got into him happened within the walls of our home. Then it became so much more than that. The nervousness escalated to such a point that the cat would hide under the daybed and not come out.

He literally had to dragged out for meals and if he did indeed eat, then nine times out of ten he would vomit the food back up. Then there were other bizarre things he was doing that were totally out of character. Like pooping in the bathtub and peeing on the floor near the toilet. For years he had used the litter pans like all the rest so what brought all this on. Well, it seems that the ceiling fan that we put in our living room scared the 'beegeeses' out of the little critter so he avoided walking past it to where the litter pans were. Get it? That problem was solvable. The eating problem wasn't as easy to deal with but eventually we found some solutions for that too.

Through it all and there was lots to go through, one thing never changed and that his love for his mother. Again with the unique pet situation. He adores her and he loved Rory too, they formed a great friendship, Mother's boy and another boy.

Scaredy Cat!

Robbie is to say the least, unusual. I brought him home to my wife on a hot August day a dozen years ago. His owner picked him out of a crowd of cats that she feeds and houses out in the country. She said she thought there was something special about him and there was. Robbie is a beige cat with white markings or a white cat with beige markings, whichever way you look at him. His tail is striped., I am sure of that. He also has a goatee which makes him in his own way, handsome.

I named him after my best friend for the same reason someone would name a child after someone, because I love him. He even came along with me and his namesake for Robbie's first check-up at the vet. Robbie had to be vaccinated against feline-leukemia because another of our house-cats is living with that disease. The first few weeks Robbie lived a sequestered life in our living room with the door closed to the rest of the house. Until a cat is twelve weeks old the vaccine does not take effect. This is a necessary precaution that we are forced to take in order to sustain the lives of our pets.

Robbie made the best of the situation. It was easy to see that he made himself at home. He was able to amuse himself by getting into absolutely everything, squeeze into tight places, climb the drapes and sleep ever so comfortably in a sunbeam. I said it before and I'll say it again. Everything I ever learned about comfort I have learned from a cat.

When the doors were finally open he ran freely throughout the house and interacted with our two other cats. Rory loved his new playmate and they seem to hit it off right away. India was not amused. Not only did she not like this newcomer, she thought that she might lose her place as Queen of the Castle. Not a chance! Robbie soon learned who not to bother and who to bother with. His first love is Mother. She is the food lady. She is the one who talks soft and sweet and holds the baby boy and kisses and brushes him and kisses some more. Mother loves Robbie and Robbie loves Mother.

After a year or two of living this quiet and comfortable indoor life something happened. I am not sure quite what it was. After several visits to the vet because of an ear infection, Robbie's behaviour started to change. He seemed skittish and nervous all the time. Often he would run from the room the moment one of us entered. He was no longer affectionate and quite often distant. He found refuge under our daybed in the den. Amid the boxes and cartons stored under there was the solace he so badly required. It was quiet under there and dark too. This seemed to be the only place where he found comfort. Hours and hours at first and then days on end. He would only come out for meals. Sometimes he didn't even do that. In the event that he did come out he nervously sat waiting for his food and then promptly returned to the safety and security underneath the day bed. Most people didn't even know we had a third cat because no one ever saw him. I imagined that he had a whole secret world under there. I would even write about it for the kids I work with but secretly I was scared.

Robbie was losing weight and looking pale. I guess frail would be the word. He started to vomit his meals. First I thought we gave him too much, and then I thought maybe he was allergic to the food. He would not consume human food at all. He had no desire for bacon or bologna, something the other two cats would have killed for. Eating and vomiting was becoming a daily occurrence. I feared for his tender little life. Then there was the behaviour problem. Robbie was not using the litter pan. Instead he would deposit his stool in the bathtub or on the floor between the tub and wall.

Off to the vet several times proved useless. During the visits the amount of fur that would fall off his trembling body made me sick to my stomach. I loved the little guy yet it was easy to see that he was starving himself to death. The vet told us that it may have been the ear infection causing this nervousness. Perhaps during an ear cleaning his ear drum was damaged. If so then the sound of mere scuffing of feet would sound like thunder to him. Eating crunchy food might too add to his discomfort therefore upsetting his stomach and as a result vomiting.

Had it not been for Sherry's diligence Robbie might very well be a thing of the past. My wife is a serious pet owner. She does whatever she has to, to take proper care of her pets. Since Robbie wasn't himself she would try her best to comfort him. The quest was on the save his precious life. If we were able to catch him Robbie and Mommy would spend some quiet time alone in a room with the door closed. He liked that. It was during one of those times that Mommy discovered a solution to one of his problems. There was something about the ceiling fan that scared him. Since you had to pass by the living room to get to the spare room where the litter pans are it was easier to stay at the other end of the house. He held it in for as long as he could and then finally had to let it out. Literally! So the solution to that was to give him his own litter box at the other end of the house.

Due to ill health Robbie's teeth had a big build-up of tartar and that's not a good thing. Dental Diet is a crunchy food product designed to clean a cat's teeth while also providing them with a tasty snack. This is something Robbie liked and enjoyed. That consumption of food was the only thing that would stay in his stomach. I also suggested to Sherry that after eating toast in the morning to place a drop of milk on the remaining crumbs and allow him to lick it up. This would give him calcium and fibre but also not make him sick. Perhaps the milk coated his stomach and settled it a little. Who knows? He seemed to improve. With the better health came bravery and courage. He started to come out from under the daybed more often and see what was going on.

When our older cat was diagnosed with diabetes it was suggested by the vet to limit his treats and to place him on a strict diet. Not an easy thing to do. A weight control product was sent home in sample form to see if the cat would eat it. Well when you are on a diet you will eat pretty much everything that is set in front of you. But then a wonderful thing happened. Robbie was interested in the new food and seemed to like it. Well it took a while but there he was a brand new cat. Robbie has gained weight, he looks better and he stays out for hours on end. Is he still nervous? Yup! Is he still skittish? Yes, at times. But overall he is fantastic. I couldn't be prouder of Mother and her efforts on behalf of that cat.

Ladies and Gentlemen, Miss Bette Davis

When the mother cat abandoned her litter, there was no choice for the owner but to have them put down. Not courageous enough to do it herself, she relied on the talents of the vet. Two out of five were already dead upon arrival. As the doctor filled her needle to finish off what was left of the unwanted litter, one such bright eyed little amoeba lifted her head and looked straight into the face of the vet who held their very fate in her hands. In a moment true to that of the Grinch, the woman doctor had a change of heart. And so was there before her a boy named Bogart, a girl named Maple and the bright-eyed Bette Davis. Miss Davis, named for her resemblance to the famed actress that the title stuck. It turns out that the bright eyes weren't the only similarity to the screen legend. This little kitten had just as fiery a personality and was just as dramatic in her actions. No one could take their eyes off of her, especially me.

I didn't sleep much as a teen. I was up all hours of the night and dragged myself around all day. It seems with all that was going on in my life, sleep did not play a major role. Late night television was at it's best on CBC. It showed movies from the thirties and forties and I must tell you some of them were down right fantastic. I grew to admire Bogart, Clark Gable, Joan Crawford, Errol Flynn, Olivia deHavilland and Bette Davis, probably the best actress for her time. It was her movies over the others that I anticipated mostly because

I never knew what I was in for. I grew to admire her immensely. So when I stumbled across a feline with that name......well then....

I first met Bette Davis the kitten, when I dropped by the vet for some over priced cat food, and the little vixen came tearing around the corner in a flying rage, and attacked some unsuspecting leashes hanging on a nearby hook. I asked the clerk "Who's that?" They replied "Bette Davis" proudly. As quickly as she appeared she disappeared. I left the place fascinated by her.. When I went out to the car I realized that I had left something, behind, so I went back to retrieve it. There was Miss Davis again, flying around after something and determined to get what ever it was. Since she came into arm's reach I quickly swooped her up in one hand and looked into her face. She stared right back into mine and while I was looking at her with adoring eyes, she leaned over and bit me square on the nose. It was right then and there that I fell in love with Miss Bette Davis. I simply had to have her and I told the clerk so.

They were quick to explain that the little tyke had been promised to someone else. My answer to that was "Do you even know who I am? I always get what I want." All laughed and I was on my way. My wife, for once, stayed in the car and so I spent the rest of the evening telling her about the little kitten that was so small that she fit into the palm of my hand, and I proceeded to tell her about the richness of her eyes and just how spunky she was. I don't think I ever wanted anything so much in my life as I did that kitten, but I guess it wasn't meant to be.

A day or so later, a message was on the phone from Juanita at the vet saying that the lady had changed her mind about taking Bette, and if I still wanted her, she was there. I called Sherry and told her about the call, and she said when she got home, we would sit down and discuss it. I left our apartment on Prince Street and immediately drove down to the vet and there she was, my little vixen, Bette Davis, my little cat, my little kitten and the newest member of our ever expanding family. By the time I got home with Bette, there was Sherry standing at the top of the stairs. She took little notice of the bump in my tee-shirt until it moved. Looking at me scornfully she said "I thought we were going to talk about it?" It was at that moment that Miss Davis popped her head out the neck of my shirt and said hello to her new Mother. Sherry was hooked.

So, there was Rory, the Gentle Giant, India, Queen of the Castle, Robbie, the Scaredy Cat and now, Miss Bette Davis, the greatest dramatic cat actress in the world. They became known as the Four Cats of Prince Street and their lives are each unique and interesting stories. I should know, I write those very stories and have lived what I write. That's all coming up a little later.

She's So Unusual

Bette Davis, is to say the least, unusual. This year she turns fourteen and although that makes her a senior citizen, she still resembles a kitten. Smaller than the others in our household, this little vixen can hold her own. She rules the upstairs, quite often putting the run to the others for no other reason than they bothered her.

Bette Davis is as dramatic as the actress she is named after. While our version may never win an Academy Award, she is certainly the star of our show. She asks for nothing. Well, I shouldn't say that. When she wants something she is the kindest, cuddliest and cutest girl in the world. It is very hard to resist her demands. All she ever wants is a little handful of food, a mouse-full to be exact. Or she presents herself to the empty kitchen sink so that you might run a small stream of dripping water for first, her bath, second, a drink, and third, so she can play. She even has this habit of letting the water drip on her head. She's so unusual. While Bette loves water, most cats don't. If she could talk she would tell you she is not like most cats.

Bette Davis would tell you that in so many words, if she ever had anything to say that is. She does not meow. Some cats don't and she is one of them. She speaks volumes with her movements and her sudden interest in you. Therefore when she "speaks" I listen. I wish the others were that quiet.

Bette Davis has never been outside. Not only is she an indoor cat but she prefers it that way. Not one for cold winds or snow, she would much rather spend her time in a sunbeam or in Mother's and

Father's bed. She tends to make the most of any situation. Comfort first, and then sleep.

Bette Davis loves her Daddy. He is interesting enough to follow through the house both upstairs and down. He is someone who likes music so Bette sits on a window sill and watches him make a fool of himself dancing around the den with his headphones on. Still, it's nice for both of them.

Bette Davis is a loner. There are several reasons why a cat might prefer to be alone. Independence! Yeah, that's one. Hateful! Yeah, that's another. She had made such enemies of the other felines that I think when we go to work; the others gang up on her. At least she is able to convince her Daddy that the others are mistreating her. That way she gets carried to the kitchen for a treat. Nice kitty! Poor Baby!

Bette Davis has had her portrait done by a local artist, Robb Scott. People have raved about it. Bette doesn't care. She is well aware of how beautiful she is. She belongs on a pedestal. Perhaps that's why her bed in on top of the book case in our bedroom, so she can look down on the world. This way she can survey her kingdom.

Bette Davis can tell time. She knows when it is time to get up so she makes her way down from the basket, makes her way up the bed to Daddy and sits directly on his chest, giving a head butt or two. If he is snoring too loudly, she might even put her paw in his mouth, that will wake him up for sure. If it happens to be the weekend and Daddy insists on sleeping in, then the best thing for Bette to do is to find a comfortable spot on him somewhere and have a bath. Daddy doesn't mind that, he can sleep through anything.

And finally, Bette Davis is a thief. She has stolen my heart. She has ingratiated herself into my personal space, forced me to rearrange my thoughts and cemented a paw print on my heart. She is someone I cannot resist and am flattered that she chose me to be her personal servant. It really is an honour. Oh dear, is it nap time already? I think I need someone to cuddle with.

Straight Clean & Simple

Communication between pets and people and between people and people are both personal and interesting to observe. For instance, a mother and child can speak a language that only each other can understand. The same could be said between loving pet owners and their "children".

Bette is such a creature. She brought with her, her own determined personality and iron will. Bette Davis is a fitting name for such a persona because she is just like her namesake, the mousy, pop-eyed actress. Affection has to be on her terms and she only eats when and what she feels like. But, if she likes you she lets you know it.

None of our cats go outside. They have lived their entire lives indoors and none have a complaint about the whole process. At least, none of them have ever said so. They make the most of a sunbeam; occupy the bed with or without you in it and they take liberties that only a dog could ever dream of. Once, in school, one of the kids asked me my thoughts on what a cat's perspective of life was. "Well, I guess if we were in their shoes, we would see what the world looks like from less than a foot tall!" a pretty good answer don't you think?

A spray bottle can be a dream comes true for any pet owner. Cats hate water! If a cat gets into something it shouldn't, simply shaking the bottle will cause the culprit to exit the room quickly. Not Bette, she takes the sprays of water head on and then uses the moisture later to take a bath. This is sheer stubbornness on her part.

In fact, she loves water so much that she immediately gets into our stainless steel sink after we do the dishes. I think she likes the warmth left from the water. If there is a drip left in the tap then it is an opportunity to have a refreshing drink, but if not that purpose, she might just sit there and allow the dripping faucet to do just that on her head. I don't know why, she just does. This is what is known as a "Betty Bath".

She only eats what she likes. If you are trying to share bacon or bologna with her then they have to be "Bette Bites", a term that means small and delicate bite-size pieces that a delicate little cat can enjoy.

She sleeps when she is tired. When she is tired, she makes it known to you that it's time to retire by wrapping her tail around your legs. Her sleepy face is endearing and her feminine ways, alluring. That means it's "Bette Bye" time. Under the covers she goes. When either her mother or I enter the room at anytime of day and see the impression left in the blanket, it is known as a "Bette Bump".

This set of terms has become part of the Canton household, along with "Bette Boop" which does not refer to the comic strip, rather a dainty and soft trot across the floor. So light in the loafers that I am sure she wouldn't leave footprints in the sand.

"Bette Butt" refers to how softly yet firmly she butts her head into yours to get your undivided attention and it can also refer to a tiny and dainty behind, but let's not go there. So, have you caught on yet to just how much that girl has touched our lives? I hope so, because I believe that when something in front of you is so very straight, clean and simple, then it should be shared with the world.

Ladies and Gentlemen, the most dramatic cat actress in the world has chosen my wife and me as her life assignment, Miss Bette Davis!

For the Love of Me

It takes a good man to accept another man's child as his own. This is usually accomplished by a deepening affection for the mother. As a result the child grows on you. I knew if my wife and I never had children then it would be highly unlikely that I would ever hold another man's baby and call it my own. In the unlikely event that it did happen, it would probably have to be Chinese and the natural parents would have to be way around the world. I couldn't have them living next door.

Well, recently such a thing happened to me. An oriental family had a baby that needed a decent home and parents. We had to be checked out and we had to pay a fortune, but finally the void that exists inside me has found a purpose.

When I first looked into the little girl's face, I knew I had to be accepting that she wasn't like me and my wife. I had to accept that she wasn't like the other kids in my neighborhood but what overcame me was a true sense of love. This little girl was a gift from God. Through circumstances beyond my control, she found her way into our lives and into my heart.

Our lives were turned upside down at her arrival, and since she had to secure a place in our family to last a lifetime, she turned those eyes to me. I want you to remember something, I am only human and I had every intention of facing my responsibilities, like any good man. What I didn't know was just how deep my feelings ran. I am realizing all that now.

This little rose that found her way to me has realized that she owns my embrace, she controls my affection, she's made me grow and she contributes to my well being by loving me in return, just as much as I love her.

Is she another man's child, nope! She's mine for a lifetime. I will do my best to protect her from the harshness of the real world, pick her up when she falls, or allow her to pick herself up when she falls, no matter how much it hurts me. I want her to be strong and yet I feel protective too. I will listen to her and talk to her and accept her for who she is. I know she's not perfect, but to me she is wonderful, I wouldn't change a thing. She makes me happy when I am around her and every day after school we have few moments together catching up on our day.

January 24th is her birthday, Happy Birthday Rozie the dog! A sh'tzu, I love you.

Speaking of dogs. In the early days when our family was just beginning, and our sister Joan was quite young, she would venture across the street everyday to our grandparents. The Cantons were a large family and each and every one of them contributed something to the running of the farm at 16 Russell. Uncle Ken, the youngest of the lot was a mere nine years older than Joan at the time. He was terribly upset that his dog Freckles had passed away. Joan who was five years old could not see what the fuss was all about. "Just fro him in the dump" "He's no good now, just fro him in the dump." Apparently, anything our mother tried to do to quiet Joan down was futile. Poor Uncle Ken. I am sure he could've killed her. Lol!

Just So You Know....

When we moved into our neighbourhood I got to know some very interesting people. Those that come to mind first are our neighbours across the street, Faye and Paul. She, a school teacher and he, her devoted husband, are both educated and interesting. They have an only child, a son, Ben, a rosy cheeked and mannerly little boy. At the time we moved into the neighbourhood, they also had a dog, a black lab named Barney. This was her dog.

When Faye's dog Barney had to be put down, I was sad. Such a loss, I thought to myself. I was wrong. It was devastating for Faye. This kind and wonderful woman suffered in silence at her loss probably thinking no one would ever understand. Her husband Paul did. He watched her go through the motions of grief and in an attempt to make her feel better, he brought her a puppy. Another black lab named Mindy.

We, the Cantons, had only cats for pets; I could never see us having a dog, too much work I thought. It seems I was mistaken. My wife Sherry insisted we get ourselves a dog and so we did. In doing so, I never thought I would ever care for something so, so canine. I was wrong. I love my dog. She, Rozie, has an immense amount of affection for me and me for her. I am now, to say the least, complete. Just so you know.

Faye is an honest woman. She tells the truth where this dog is concerned. Mindy is a pet. Her heart has never completely healed where Barney is concerned and truthfully, it never will. Oh don't get me wrong, she likes the dog. Faye likes all living things and she respects the world around her, but please don't ask her to put her heart on the line anytime soon. She still has some healing to do. Just so you know.

Mindy is a wonderful dog. She's playful and cuddly, or should I say she's as good a dog as she can be. A little clumsy and awkward, she's simply lovely. We, the Cantons think so. We babysit her while the family is away. We watch over their home for them and we take care of their pet. Or does she take care of us? We love her! Just so you know.

Mindy likes to come and visit. She adores my wife Sherry and she likes our dog, Rozie. Now Rozie on the other hand, tolerates Mindy. She is very happy when she visits but just as happy when she leaves. It's a spoiled brat sort of thing. Rozie wants everyone to remember that this is her house!

Mindy makes herself at home in our house. She writhes on the carpet, follows my wife around while she is cooking, plays with Rozie and lies comfortably at my feet while I watch TV. But every so often, finds her way to the window to see if her family is home yet. It's easy to see that she loves each and every one of them. Mindy has a nice life there. She makes the most of her backyard, great for digging. She loves the shade of the trees in summer and the taste of snow in her snout in winter. It really is a great place to live. She loves her life and she loves her neighbours. What more could a dog ask for?

So, as these things go, I take a moment out of my busy life to look around me and to take the time to appreciate where I live. I take the time to appreciate who I live with and am inspired by a dog across the street, looking out the living room window, surveying her kingdom and wagging a tail because the neighbours are home. It makes a man feel good, you know. Considering all the miserable things that are going on in the world, we have a good thing going here.

You see, Paul didn't just give his wife a gift when he put Mindy on her desk at school, he gave us a gift as well. I now share this wonderful gift with all of you and that, Ladies and Gentlemen, is a wonderful thing, just so you know.

P. S. Since the printing of this story Mindy has passed away. I am only the neighbor who babysat her for the past nine years and I must tell you, I was heart-broken. Still, like most things in life, there was not much I could do about it. Later on the family decided to purchase a new dog, a beagle and although I have grown very fond of her, I was still hurting over the loss of the other so I kept my distance. Well, when a photo arrived with the new dog reading my book Russell Street Memories, I at least had to give her a chance. After all, if she is smart enough to read then I might as well give her a minute of my time. All is well once again. In some ways I am so very happy to meet Marcy and to move forward. But, like so many other soft hearted guys, I still miss the one that crossed over.

Jack Rabbit

This story is part of a series of stories for young hearts and was inspired by a boy I knew with big ears....

When they're born they call them bunnies and when they're grown they call them rabbits, that's just the way it is. Growing up on the Tantarmar marshes was very interesting to this particular clutch of bunnies. There are always lots to do, lots to see and lots of others to play with. Generations of our family lived on the marsh, our grandparents, our parents and us. It is great to have family around because it is from them that you learn how to survive in this world. Our mother took care of all of us and there were lots of us too and it seemed we all looked alike and I guess that's okay. All in all it was a happy life, no one ever thought of leaving the marsh but things change when you grow up.

One day a bunny from away dropped by to play and he was interesting to us because he seemed to know so much more than we did. He traveled a lot and saw lots more of our vast marsh than we ever did. I guess in a way it made him more worldly and sophisticated. As we were all busy running around playing and jumping he took a long look at us and said "Who's that?" pointing to my brother Jack. "He sure does have big ears". Now this came as a bit of a shock as we never really noticed the fact that Jack had big ears until this stranger pointed it out, but Jack did indeed have bigger ears than all of us. Realizing this was not funny rather sad to know that this made Jack different from the rest of us. We didn't want him to feel different, or to have his feelings hurt, he was after all, our brother.

In my heart I was sad because this stranger was making fun of one of us so I went to talk to Mother about it. She explained the whole situation to me knowing very well how upset I got over things like that. Jack looks the way he does for a reason, he inherited his look. "Who is the greatest man you know?" she asked and I was quick to reply "Grampie" and he was. "Well take a look at his ears sometime, he has big ears too so you don't have to worry about Jack, he will be fine, after all he is carrying on a family tradition." And he is.

Winters can be wicked on the marsh that's why we all have to cuddle. Our mother keeps us very close and that is a nice feeling. Heavy snowfall blows in over the marsh covering everything in it's path. It's great to play in. Summers are warm and nice. This summer was a particularly dry one. This worries Mother although she never talks about it. She just stares out into the horizon watching first at sunrise and then at sunset. I could feel the twigs snap beneath my feet as I walked along the trail. We knew never to venture very far from our mother or she would come and get us and bring us back. All she ever wanted was for us to be safe. When I went down to the river for a drink I was surprised to find it had gone dry. This never happens but as I said this summer was a dry one.

As the warm breeze blew gently across the marsh there was in the distance the usual clatter from our friends and neighbors, other bunnies our age running and jumping and playing. From behind me off in the distance I could see Jack running toward us. He had look of sheer terror on his face. He flew past me and the others and ran right to our mother. With one word from his mouth our lives would change forever. Fire!

My mother stomped her foot three times. This was not a test it was the real thing. In an instant we as a family came together and flew as quickly as we could off the marsh and up the field and ran and ran until our mother was sure that we were safe. My heart was beating so loudly in my ears that I could not see or hear clearly. I was frightened for my life and for good reason. The fire spread quickly over the entire marsh and destroyed everything in its path.

Homes were gone, food, and unfortunately some lives too. But our mother had brought all of her bunnies to safety and as we looked at all the devastation on the marsh and up at the smoke-filled sky we knew that we were alive because our brother Jack, the one with the big ears, heard the crackling of the fire before anyone else did and ran to warn our mother. Jack Rabbit saved the day.

Ok, so there wasn't a cat or a dog in the story, but it is still cute don't you think!

Looking for Love

When a person takes home a puppy or a kitten they have to realize that they are taking on a huge responsibility. They must accept the fact that this little face requires some serious attention. It would also be great if one were to realize that this is a privilege and one that requires sacrifice on your part. In return for all this effort you will receive unconditional love, friendship and a devoted companion who only has eyes for you. That's the privilege part.

When my wife insisted on getting a dog, I protested loudly. You know the drill. "A dog is more responsibility than I can handle, I'm too busy to properly care for it and besides I work a lot! The answer is NO!"

So we got one. Friends and relatives whispered that this was a replacement for a child. Others always seem to know you better than you know yourself. Whatever!

This particular relationship between man and beast has turned out to be quite an adventure. My little dog came with an invisible label around her neck that said "looking for love". And I tell you, she's found it.

It took me only a moment to see how special she is, but it took the first year for her to permanently embed herself into my soul. She sits in the window waiting for me, she naps when I do, she loves me whether or not I smell clean and fresh, and she'd even let me share my food with her if I would like to. What more, ladies and gentlemen, could a man ask for?

So, if I were to take my thoughts and feelings and put them into words on this page, I would have to start by thanking God for sending her to me, thank my mother for teaching me about the beauty that exists here before our eyes, and thank my father for being too gentle a soul to ever kill a deer despite numerous hunting trips. I inherited that gene from him.

So, I will end this today with this request. Take the time to stop and enjoy the beauty around you, pat your dog on the head and be grateful that you have such a loyal friend and urge friends and family to have their pets spayed or neutered. Just because.

Baby Dog

I never wanted a dog! Too much work I said to myself. I feel that it is too much responsibility taking it indoors and outdoors all the time. Even if I did I could never have the one dog I wanted, Elizabeth, a cocker spaniel from the Disney movie Pollyanna. She is someone I fell in love with years ago and I would often state that if I ever had a dog, I would want an Elizabeth.

The cats were pet enough. After all there were five of them and they certainly kept us from feeling lonely and they certainly were ideal and indoor house-pets. So what's the problem? Well, my wife is the problem. She wanted a dog. She desperately wanted a dog and so guess what? We got one! On May 11 she brought home a tri-coloured Sh'tzu (I am sure you don't spell it that way!) The poor little thing! There she was, fresh from the orphanage and shy to just about everything; she just laid there and quietly looked around. No bigger than my two hands cupped, I must say she was a pretty little thing but let's face it, she was no Elizabeth.

The cats were not amused. Most of them had never even seen a dog before and those who did were terrified. Those except India, my black cat, well, she was totally miffed. At 14 years of age she is undoubtedly the Queen of the Castle and as far a she was concerned that thing just had to go. I tried to reason with her, to appeal to her sensitive side, but to no avail. She went off sulking as usual and over time we figured she would come around. Well, I'll let you know if that ever happens.

I named the dog Rozie, after Rosie O'Donnell and I thought that was deemed appropriate. So there before me was Rozie Macdonald Canton, our Rose, our baby, our baby dog. I cannot lie, I was falling in love with her and she with me. I didn't know exactly what to do with her so I would just take and kiss her and talk to her and love her. She enjoyed the attention and affection and she returned it tenfold. India watched from the sidelines with a look of sheer disgust on her face and in her attitude. Whatever!

Dogs need routine. So in order to train her the way you should we used a crate. This is a dog cage large enough to house the dog comfortably. By comfortably I mean, with a large puff and some stuffed animals for company. As long as the crate was facing us, our baby dog would settle in comfortably and amazingly sleep the entire night. Early in the morning my wife would take Rozie outside to do her business and then return her to our bedroom and place her onto the bed with Daddy. This gave my wife a chance to get ready for work in her own good time.

Rozie would lay on the end of the bed just as quiet as a mouse until she could feel Daddy stir. Then the antics would begin. Now that Daddy was awake it was time for a tickle and some kissing and wrestling. Rozie always like that and so did Daddy. On those mornings that Daddy might get a chance to sleep in, Rozie would do her best to be quiet but it wasn't easy. So, she would crawl on her belly and inch her way up to be near Daddy's face. If I laid there with my eyes closed I could feel her breath on my cheek, she was so close. Then when I opened an eye the games would begin.

Just as routine as the sleeping arrangements were the eating habits. It is important to feed the dog around the same time every day. Like I said, routine. And don't feed them table scraps. If you start you will never break the habit. You don't want a beggar at the table at every meal. Also, these dogs are very sensitive so food other than their own can upset their stomachs.

India, who always slept in the bed on or near Daddy, refused to give up her rightful place to that dog or any animal. She was the original Daddy's girl and no one and nothing was going to take that away from her. So, boundaries had to be established and once they were and the hissing and growling was through, India knew her place and Rozie knew hers. I just stayed in the middle.

Dogs such as these require a decent amount of maintenance so off to the dog-groomer we go. A nice lady named Joan clips the dog's nails, trims her ears, clips around her eyes, and pricks her ears and brushes out her easily matted coat. Since we were headed into yet another hot summer we decided to have Rozie shaved down and her look was totally different from when I took her in. She looked more like a cocker spaniel than a sh'tzu but it was still our baby dog. So after all of the fuss I had my Elizabeth, Elizabeth Rose, she was just wearing someone else's fur coat.

So onward we went over the next year and a half with little or no fanfare. Rozie is happy here with us, the cats seemed to have accepted her and India, well, that's another story!

You Needed Me!

Dear Anne Murray:

Well I must tell you, I've finally got it. I finally understand the meaning of that song and not in the way you think, I am sure. And it's only taken thirty years. So here goes.

I would never have picked that song. If I had, I don't think I would have released it as a single. I would have recorded it, it's a good song. I probably would've buried it somewhere in an album hoping someone would see its potential down the road. You saw something in that song and pushed for it, and the whole world is glad you did. Engagements, weddings, funerals, it seems that song has a place at every table. That in itself is a wonderful thing. But really, not for me.

I am the lucky one. I have a real sense of who I am. I know what true love is, I found it at an early age. I knew as a teenager that Sherry would be my wife and she is. I cannot ever see me married to anyone but her for many reasons, but mostly it wouldn't be fair to compare. I don't lack a lot in my life as it is a pretty full one. I work in a junior high school and as a waiter, I write, I host a local talk show and it gets good returns. I live in a nice neighbourhood in a house that is nearly paid for, and as a result I am a happy man. My wife has turned our house into a home and turned this boy into a man. She's the type that makes you want to be a better person. She didn't need me for that; it's just the way it is. Recently, the two of us, the Todd and Sherry Cantons, celebrated our 25th wedding anniversary. Not a surprise to me, I knew we would make it, I just ask for a million more.

We have no children. My wife never felt she had any maternal instincts and I never pushed for it. It seems that I didn't need anything to fill me as I never seem to feel empty. But every once in a while I think to myself, wouldn't it be something to see what Sherry and I could create, and yet, it was okay for just the two of us. It's always been okay for the two of us. My family never got it, but then they never got the whole "Anne Murray" thing either. Too bad for them.

We live with four indoor house-cats and a dog. I never wanted a dog. Too much work I thought. I was wrong. She, Rozie, a sh'tzu, has rearranged my life in a very positive way. She likes me for who I am and in return I shower her with all the love and affection I can muster. It really is a nice feeling when I come home at night and it is announced that I have arrived. I get that greeting every time. Lately I find I am sticking closer to home because of her, and that's a nice thing as well. That is until she got sick.

She required dental surgery. Her teeth had to be cleaned, and if necessary, an extraction or two. Pretty routine stuff, or so I thought. Then the Doctor called nothing to worry about. "Did you know your dog had headaches?" Huh? No I did not, how would you know? Well, growling, irritable, moody. She is none of these things. (She is the gentlest, kindest element of my private life). It seems an infected tooth got pushed up into her sinuses. Ouch! The problem was taken care of and she would soon be ready to go home.

When I walked into the office and past the receptionist I was greeted with the familiar smells of a veterinary hospital and there she was, my baby girl, all drugged up, drooling, and droopy. Still that tail gave a familiar wag. She loves me. That's all there is to it, she loves me and I love her. I carried her out to the car and drove slowly home. She was ready for bed. I looked at her tiny little tired face and as she placed her head on my lap, it occurred to me. You are where you belong, in a safe and comfortable home. You have a Daddy that loves you. You Needed Me! Or I guess I needed you. I talked to God one time about a baby and he gave me an angel instead.

Despite my independence, my modern thinking, my way of looking at the world, my philosophies great and small and me, I have finally realized that life really is worth living, love is all a person needs to inspire and motivate them, and that no matter how old a person gets, there is still something inside of you to give. I intend to keep on giving, loving, and laughing, what else on earth, is there?

Love to you and your family,

Take care and be well and as I have always said where you and your music are concerned "Quality never goes out of style"

P. S. I have been an Anne Murray fan since forever. I do not remember a time in my life where her music did not exist. It is only fitting that she be a part of a loving tribute to something I hold so dear to my heart, the animal kingdom and all it has to offer.

Bird Brain

The little black and white bird sat alone on a branch reading a book. His glasses kept slipping off the end of his beak. All of the other birdies used to make fun of Rudolph because he was a bookworm (not an affectionate name in the bird kingdom). At times he was referred to as a Bird Brain. Well, that's exactly what he was. A brain. While the rest of the young birds were off somewhere doing who knows what, Rudolph would sit and read about the wonders of the world. He quite often could be found deep in thought .

One day, like many days, Horace the cat decided to climb the tree and get a closer look at Rudolph. This, of course, would make any bird nervous but not our little birdbrain. He would wait until Horace was almost upon him and then whoosh! He would fly away. The rest of the little birds ran home to their mothers when Horace was about but not our little birdbrain. Rudolph would just flap about laughing. Horace did not see the humour in all of this. After so many futile attempts to catch Rudolph, Horace thought maybe he could sweet talk him into coming near. Again Rudolph would allow Horace to get close and then again at the last moment he would escape.

In the eyes of the little birds Rudolph should have been viewed as a brave little hero for his daring feats but instead they saw it as a death wish. Fooling around with Horace was only going to get you one place and that was dead. Rudolph was shunned more than ever. It didn't seem to bother him. Well at least it looked that way.

What did he care about those silly little birds anyway, such juveniles. Some day he would show them!

That day came last Saturday when Horace once again climbed the tree in hopes of getting a chance at Rudolph. Today the little birdbrain was dancing about on the end of a branch singing out "I have a secret". He would bounce about shaking his head back and forth when the unexpected happened. His glasses fell off of his head. This left him nearly blind. As he stumbled about feeling around for his glasses Horace the cat was silently gaining on him. Rudolph moved about quite disoriented and disappeared out of view of Horace just for a moment. He spotted Rudolph back on and pounced. All that flew about was feathers. The other birds let out shrieks and cries for the loss of one of their own. Then it all came to light and much to Horace's shock it was not Rudolph at all. It was merely feathers and glue carefully and cleverly put together by Rudolph. Horace had a heck of a time spitting out paste and feathers while trying not to lose his grip on the branch. In utter frustration Horace the cat went on his way totally ticked off. From where he was hiding all the little birdbrain could do was laugh.

But it was when his mother realized that he had used her good feathers for this nasty trick she took Rudolph by the wing and marched him home stopping once to give him a spanking. The rest of the little birdies just shook their heads and thought to themselves, what a bird brain, and they were absolutely right! Rudolph's mother sent him to bed early and although he knew it was a nasty trick to play on one and all the little birdbrain couldn't help but chuckle to himself. I guess one should never assume.....

Rory Loves Sara

When my sister Ruth asked me to be Godfather to her daughter Sara I must say that I was, to say the least, proud. The real honour has been watching that girl grow into the fine upstanding young woman she is today. I suspect though, she will always be a little girl to me.

Rory the cat has seen a lot over the years. His first home was at Anne and Ruth's house in Dartmouth. He was a kitten then. Sara Canton was just a little girl when her mother brought him home as a pet. Sara's cousin Danny named him Rory after his own childhood nickname. The name stuck. Rory was an adorable Maine Coon kitten, playful and friendly and very orange. It was not his nature to scratch or bite.

He loved Sara very much and became her constant companion. Often times he would perform for her by doing tricks that he had learned but his favourite was cramming himself into small spaces. There was a round fish bowl that he was able to cram his whole body into. When you first looked at it you might think that there was an orange sweater in the bowl until it would blink its eyes, that's when you would have to take a better look. Rory liked to play that's for sure. Even an empty beer case was a good place to in which to stuff yourself. First it was a six-pack box but he soon out grew that and into a dozen case. There was one item in the house that he especially enjoyed and that was the water bed. He could see the ripples in the mattress and he tried his best to catch one but instead his natural predator instincts were about to get him into trouble because his developing claws were leaving very thin scratches in which water was able to leak out. This didn't thrill Sara's mother Ruth. After all it was her water bed that he was doing this to.

He also liked to hide under things like newspapers. To him it was like being in a tent. He would often stay there for hours not moving a whisker. Now while this was a fun game for Rory it was not always amusing to the person who was trying to read the paper. He was getting so big that five year old Sara couldn't always carry him without his legs dragging on the floor but that was fine with him as he always enjoyed it when Sara would put her arms around him. He loved her very much. Sara was soon realizing that Rory was her closest companion but this rang true on the day he disappeared. Sara was beside herself with worry and she was unable to stop crying. She cried in such a way that her tears would squirt out like when you squeeze the juice out of a grapefruit. Ruth tried to settle her down but nothing seemed to work so Ruth did what came natural to her, she called Gram in Amherst.

The one thing about Gram was that she had a good understanding of little people and when a problem arose, Gram could quite often come up with a solution. Today was no exception. She told Sara over the phone to call Rory's name and to listen very carefully and very quietly to see if he would answer. She tried it but it seemed hopeless. Gram told her to do it one more time. Sara could hear something but what was it? It was the quietest little peep. It seems that Rory had been taking a nap in the laundry basket while Ruth was doing the wash. Once the first load of clothes was done in the dryer Ruth placed the warm clothes on the basket on top of Rory without realizing it. Since he enjoyed the warmth he just stayed put. A couple of hours went by. It was when he heard Sara calling his name that he sprang to life or at least tried to. The weight of the clothes held him in place so all he could do was yell and that was what she heard. Ruth and Sara came to the rescue and the two friends were reunited.

As time passed and Anne and Ruth were forced to move the only place available was a building that did not allow pets. It seems that they had to give Rory up but certainly would not do so unless it was to a good home. Ruth called her brother Todd in Truro and asked if he and his wife Sherry would be able to accommodate Rory by taking him in. Ruth had remembered an earlier visit from Todd and Sherry in which Sherry showed great interest in Rory so she knew that if he did move to Truro that he would be properly taken care of. That is how The Cats of Prince Street came to be. Rory was the first, the king of beasts. Our big beautiful lion will be fourteen soon and he is one majestic looking specimen. He is the one who greets you from the top of the stairs when you come in and has welcomed all the other cats into our family and has created a bond with each and every one of them; India, Angel, Robbie and Bette. He has proven to be a gentle giant and a gentleman of cats.

Life with Rory certainly has been inspiring but not as much as the day a couple of years later that Sara had dropped in on her way to Amherst to see Gram. While the other cats were anxious to inspect Ruth and Anne, Rory just stayed down the hall with Sara. I called him several times for a treat but he wouldn't budge. There are a few things in this life that we are unable to explain and love is certainly one of them. Really Rory shouldn't have even remembered her but who is it for me to say. From the expression on his face and from the sound of his purring I could tell that he was content being reunited with his very special friend.

P.S. All of us cats and dogs alike miss Gram and her helpful advice no matter how old we get.

I'll Never Love Anyone

I'll never love anyone like I love my cat India. While she may not be the most gorgeous cat in the world, to me she is beautiful. At fourteen years of age her black fur coat is soft like a kitten's and her piercing green eyes are still able to make me melt. She is very hard to resist and this is why. I bought her at a pet store for half/off because a long weekend was approaching and since she was the only one left she would have to stay there all by herself.

The clerk told me that no one wanted her as she was the runt of the litter. She was very tiny and so adorable that I just had to have her. And besides it would be great company for our grown house-cat Rory. When I walked up the steps into our apartment on Prince Street, Rory, as usual was waiting at the top of the stairs to greet me. Immediately the nose was twitching, not in anticipation of a new family member rather that look the one gets on their face when a freshly grilled T-bone steak is set in front of them.

I knew immediately that I would have to protect this little one until we all got used to each other. Our supper that evening was KFC and it was at that time that I was introduced to India's ferocious appetite, she helped herself to a drumstick and attempted to drag it across the coffee table growling fiercely at anyone who would try to take it from her. I knew right then and there that this was a feisty little critter. She took right to me and found a comfortable spot in the nape of my neck and she has successfully remained there since. Since I was the one who rescued her it was her turn to capture my heart and she did it. She followed me from room to room, sat on my lap while I watched television, slept in the bed with me, and at times has used me as a bath mat. Since she claimed me for her own personal use she was willing to protect what was hers by defending me if she had to, my protector. No one goes near her Daddy!

When I would set off for work in the morning she would lay on the floor at my feet waiting for a goodbye tickle. When I arrived home in the evening she would follow me to the bedroom while I got changed, stare at me while I was in the tub, assist me in eating my supper and lounge around with me in the evening. If I decided that I might enjoy a moment alone in my den with my headphones on India would sit outside the door and howl until I would let in. If I was unable to hear her, my wife would answer the distress call and come to her aid. She was fast becoming my constant companion.

Both my wife and I are strong animal protection. I insist on having pets spayed or neutered, providing proper care, regular visits to the vet etc. I keep my cats indoors with plenty of playroom, fresh water and open windows for fresh air and sunlight. Aren't I wonderful? I am so great that one day I insisted to my wife that we take into our home a stray half-grown kitten that had been abandoned a few streets over. She reluctantly agreed but once she saw the beautiful tigress that I named Angel she quickly came around.

While Rory immediately took to her, India's nose was out of joint at the mere thought of another cat in our house, let alone another female. In time I figured that she would come around but it seems she never did. However our house was certainly big enough for the three of them and I was glad to give that cat a clean and comfortable home. What I didn't know was that I was bringing into our very private world a deadly disease, feline leukemia. It seems that I was not quick enough in my rescue of Angel to save her completely. She lived with us in luxury for a year before succumbing to the disease. The vet told us that since Rory and India drink from the same water dish and use the same litter box they could very easily have picked up the virus.

You cannot imagine the guilt that has run through me knowing that it was me who insisted on bringing that cat home therefore putting my other two at risk. I worried about Rory the most as he and Angel had become fast friends often chasing each other from one end of our house to the other and wrestling in the process. India never went near her. Rory's test came back negative, thank God, but it was India who was susceptible and she caught it. After hearing the news I cried all day. There was no one to blame but me. Here I am at six foot three inches tall and over two hundred pounds crying over a mangy old cat who has had nothing but love and devotion to only me. My heart was breaking.

Dr. Gwen told us that some cats are able to cure themselves of this disease and after several tests we found that India still tested positive. The only thing that we could do was wait. India certainly enjoyed the extra attention and affection, (like milk on a saucer) she lapped it up. It is at the trying moments that one becomes quite humble. You see I have no children and I work a lot so I am a very busy person. I find great comfort in my baby and I honestly love her. She embraces my heart. It's been over four years since Angel had to be put down but my India is still going strong, living with her disease showing no signs progression. As we approach each New Year and all it has to offer I take the time to count my blessings, for which I am truly grateful. In fact, she is sitting on my lap as I type this looking up into my face. Daddy truly loves his baby.

Rory Story

If one does not take the time to reflect then you never know the true meaning of anything that has ever gone on in your life. True?

It's been a long time since our Gentle Giant passed away and for as long as it has been, that boy has rarely left my thoughts. Oh, I didn't sit around and cry all the time or anything like that. It's just that, like when I lost my mother, I wasn't quite ready to say goodbye.

I just don't like goodbyes. I lost my father at an early age and since it was so unexpected (to me) I have had a hard time dealing with the loss that comes along after that person is gone. Then there is also the harsh reality that all of us, no matter who we think we are, will someday pass over to the other side. Well, if I do, pass over I mean, what is over there waiting for me? Will I ever see my mother again? My father? Nan? and what about Rory? Can anyone out there guarantee that the after life offers us the explanations that man has pondered for centuries? Gee, I hope so.

When I go, I hope to have lived a full life, I hope to have had good health, I hope that all my parts are working. My father died of cancer when our mother was 43 and our mother from ALS at 71 years of age. Nana was never sick a day in her life and she died at 84 from heart complications. Rory was 14years old -losing a battle to cancerous tumours and diabetes. People say it was a long life for a cat, but, I'm afraid it just wasn't long enough. I know why people were put on this earth. I believe it was to see if survival of that species could be accomplished. It's too bad that man is quickly destroying the only home he has ever known. Animals, I believe, were put on this earth to make man think he was superior. Some were brought here to keep man company and some were sent here to humble man and believe me, it can happen.

Had the roles been reversed and Rory was the owner and I was the pet. Imagine the outcome. With his natural instincts, once I fell ill I would be abandoned or destroyed. I think he was a very caring cat and would have done his best but would eventually have had to come to a conclusion where I was concerned. I, however, as the owner, found myself compassionate and tolerant where he was concerned and as a result, fought long and hard for him. All of this was done only to lose him in the end. Oh but what a journey.

That cat had done an awful lot in his life. He was born in the city of Halifax and he and his siblings were placed in a pet store for sale. Rory was purchased for a little girl named Sara who bonded with the cat right away. He lived with Sara and her mother for a couple of years and then before coming to Truro. During that time in the city by the sea, he lived indoors as well as out and I am sure experienced a lot in doing so. This is where I think he acquired his immense love of seafood. I am also quite sure he fathered a few litters in the neighbourhood. The recipients of such animals have been (I am sure) affected by the gentleness gene that raced through Rory's entire body. As he grew large and strong he simply became known as the Gentle Giant. Once the large orange cat with a plume for a tail came to live with Sherry and me it was here he found his true home.

We had our share of clashes at first but once we met in the middle, life became more satisfying for all parties involved. This was mostly due to an unexpected surprise to Rory, a mother. Sherry Canton, in her trademark of quiet diversity, opened her heart and soul to that boy. She embraced him as though he was a child and in fact, I guess he was, her child, her boy, her friend. When he was hungry, she fed him, when he was dirty she cleaned him, when he was sick, she doctored him, and when he was gone she longed for him. Longed for and loved in such a deeply fashion that I dare say, I would not have been surprised if she had passed away from a genuinely broken heart. Had it not been for other family responsibilities, she might very well have. That's kind of how I felt when my mother died, my father, Nan and all of the rest who were gone long before I ever tired of them. A long before I was ready to say goodbye.

So will heaven be a big field with flowers under a sunny sky and will I be reunited with my mother, father, Nana? Who knows? I guess just to see the face of God would be enough and to experience the glory of the angels as well. To experience first hand, the reality of heaven and all it's glory would really be sufficient, true? Or would it not really be heaven at all if I didn't at least feel the embrace that comes in the form of an orange plume wrapped around my leg, telling me, "Father, I've missed you......"

Kitty Boy Pretty Boy

When Rory passed away I must tell you, I was heartbroken. It is not easy to lose a pet that you've lived with for such a long time. And he wasn't even my favorite. He was this large (and determined) long haired Maine Coon cat that left mounds of fur on the carpet, howled while I tried to sleep, and continually scratched the furniture.. He even bit the album cover of one of my Anne Murray records! Somehow the two of us agreed to co-exist in our home together........not because I am some wonderful animal rights advocate, fantastic human being, or all around great man.......rather, my wife, Sherry, who thought of Rory as the other love of her life.

The two had a bond that could not be broken and I was witness to the adoration that flowed back and forth between them. He was gentle and playful and such a nice cat. We called him the Gentle Giant because he was so massive and yet so gentle at the same time. Rory welcomed every new pet that came into our home and before long they were all able to see him for what he was, their friend. He would drop on his side and extend a welcoming paw to show the quite often nervous and hissing newcomer that there was nothing to fear.

To make a long story short, they miss him. India knew him the longest, her whole life, 12 yrs. Then there was Robbie, Bette Davis and Paige. Each had an enormous amount of respect for Rory and each grieved in their own way. Well, that depends on who you talk to. Do animals grieve? Or do they accept the fact that one day he went out the door and never came back? Who knows? I believe as a Christian that when an animal dies it's soul goes off to heaven to be with God who sent them here in the first place. I also believe that they are never ours, they belong to the earth. We just have the privilege to care for them while they're here.

I believe that animals are put on this earth to teach man about tenderness of the heart and to prove loyalty and devotion of a different kind. You see, the human race has disappointed me on several occasions and the animal kingdom has not. But what does all this have to do with Rory? The large orange cat with a plume for a tail.

My wife is not religious and I am quite sure that she is not superstitious. She's just a sensible and realistic woman who is serious about everything in her life. Rory died and she didn't like it. Sherry had fought so hard for that cat and did not enjoy losing. I watched her suffer and I felt her pain. There was little I could do to comfort her. However, six months to the day after Rory died I was walking home from the bar when I came upon a six month old orange kitten who looked amazingly like the gentle giant. I made the mistake of patting him and he followed me home. Well, when you are drinking you don't always think clearly so for me to bring him home was one thing but when I woke up the next morning and realized what I had done, that was another. Then reality set in.

I snuck him into the house and into the bedroom. Sherry had been restless and she was more comfortable on the couch downstairs. So in the early morning when she arose she opened the bedroom door to let India out and you can imagine her shock when she saw the orange boy sitting on the landing at the top of the stairs. The same spot where Rory used to sit. Sherry probably should have screamed and she might very well have fainted if she was married to someone other than who she is. You see, this is nothing out of the ordinary for me. I brought them all home. So she burst into the bedroom and demanded an explanation as to what I thought I was doing......well, what could I say?

And so onward we went with the little boy, who looked like Rory, scratched the furniture like Rory and when introduced to Bette dropped on his side and extended his paw just the way Rory did. So, is he a reincarnation? Not likely! Or maybe, just maybe he is a gift from God telling Sherry that he loves her and that Rory is okay and for now to open her genuine heart to another kind and gentle orange boy with a plume for a tail who needs someone to take care of him.........who knows? All I know is if he bites or scratches one of my Anne Murray LP's like Rory did he's going to get it!

Robbie's Song for Jesus

Do animals have souls? When they die do they go to heaven? Opinions may vary due to religious beliefs but in general I think the consensus is yes. I can't help it, I want to know. As a Catholic it was drilled into my head that you love and honor God, your parents, friends and family and you be kind to animals and the earth. Do all this and you won't go to hell. Saint Francis of Assisi has spoken on the subject and his words have been around for just about forever. He says yes.

During a visit by their priest, I was also a visitor at my sister's house. During conversation I asked him if when animals died, do they go to heaven. "No they do not," he said, "they do not have souls."

Wrong answer!

Of course they do. Why wouldn't GOD want to be surrounded by his greatest of creations? Honestly!

That makes sense, and then after thinking about it and thinking about it, it makes perfect sense! Losing pets and humans the way I did over the years has left me full of questions that I hope, would fill the void and indelible mark left on my heart by these creatures that God so lovingly sent my way. Even the Pope John Paul II said animals go to heaven.

I am told that the last sounds an animal makes just before its death are cries to God Almighty. The same as man, an animal fears, the worst, the unknown, and will fight for his last breath hoping all the while that if this is it, then please, take me to heaven to live with you there.

When my twelve year old cat Robbie took ill recently it became quite clear that death was imminent. Sickly as a kitten, skittish and reclusive as an adult, that poor boy spent most of his life hiding under the day bed or in the closet. He was nervous and anxious, not an affectionate sort, but still a pretty good pet. One thing for sure is he loved his mother. Oh people, there's no one like Mama. She, Sherry Canton, is the type who prefers animals over people. She always did. When she was a little girl she fell in love with kitty cats and they with her. At home was Frisky, a calico with whom she held a special bond. Once, a teacher from West Highlands Elementary School called and said "We love having Sherry in our class but please tell her she can't come to school everyday with a cat wrapped around her neck."

As an adult it was a must for her to have a house full. First there was Rory, India, and Angel was only with us for a year but in that short time left a lasting impression. To this day when one of us sees a tiger striped cat we call it an "angel." To ease Sherry's heart over the loss of that cat, I brought home a beige and white kitten and plunked him down on the ironing board. At first she resisted but then she looked into the face of this delicate boy and soon she fell in love. So did he.

Then we found a broken doll and nursed her back to health. Her name is Paige, a black and white beauty. Simon, the pretty boy looked amazingly like Rory so he fit in nicely and then there's Chloe, a tortoise shell. Each comes with their own unique personalities and quirks.

Robbie's and Mommy's relationship blossomed over the years. He quite often sought her out throughout the night and would quite often cuddle with her, purring rather loudly with contentment. She purred too!

Our boy was a weak one. If left to his own devices in the wild he would have surely died as a young cat. If he had to chase after a mouse for food he would surely have starved to death. It just wasn't in his gentle nature to kill.

When he wasn't feeling a 100% he would seek her out and she would smother him with unconditional love. Who could ask for more? But this time was worse than all the other battles. This one came on fast. He suffered from dramatic weight loss, kidney failure and was a sad boy to go along with it. Since it was so stressful for Robbie to visit the vet we felt it best to just let him be comfortable until the end. Well, the end came on a Sunday morning in June, Father's Day to be exact. Sherry and I noticed that morning at breakfast that Robbie wasn't getting around well at all so we wrapped him in swaddling cloths and she lay there with him and talked to him.

I wasn't able to reach our vet as it was a weekend. I didn't want to deal with someone who was not familiar with our situation so we just did our best to keep him comfortable. During these last hours he began to talk.

Robbie has never had a lot to say. His meow is quite scratchy sounding and he really has not made more than a peep over the years. That morning was different. He told Mama some stories, while staring into her face. When it was my turn to hold him it sounded like "Noah, Nooooo ah". I knew that with this much love in the room that God was certainly present so why Noah? Well, if I remember my catechism correctly, wasn't it Noah who took care of the animals and made sure that they were safely on the Ark, ensuring a future for all? Is Noah in his own way a saint to all animals? Could be!

When that boy took his last breath it was comforting to the both of us that he was warm and comfortable right up to the very end. We accepted him for the unusual boy he was while other pet owners might not have tolerated his ways. Kind of like Jesus in a way, he wasn't like everyone else, he had his own song to sing. While not everyone accepted HIM into their lives he still made an impression that has left an indelible mark for thousands of years.

So be it! Robbie's whole life was a safe one filled with love. That's a good thing. Also, someday when the time is right, we will all meet again at a wonderful place called Rainbow Bridge. Until then he is buried in our butterfly garden in our back yard. He himself was fragile like a butterfly and tender like one too.

His mother is sitting on the deck on this warm Sunday. She tries to hide her tears for the little boy she loved so much. She tries to be brave but she's not fooling anyone. Wait a minute, there's a beautiful butterfly softly floating by. He's singing Robbie's Song for Jesus. So here we are, the two of us with one beautiful butterfly in our midst and one in our hearts.

A Pat on the Head

If you are not willing to accept pets as an important part of your family, then please don't take them home. There's valuable advice in that statement.

Living with four house-cats and dog can certainly bring it share of interesting stories. The dynamics among the group are certainly, to say the least, entertaining. Miss Bette Davis came home in my pocket. A delicate little thing she proved to us over time that she has quite a personality. Bette Davis is the leader of the pack. She is as dramatic an actress as the original. Bette patrols the upstairs and does her best to keep the others in line. Despite the fact that she is half the size, and twice the age of the others, she's still in charge.

Paige is lovely. Paige came to us after a hit and run one street over. Our broken doll took a long time to mend but she proved herself to be a survivor. I guess that had a lot to do with her spending the first half of her life outdoors because she has never lost her street savvy. However, she has enjoyed the comfort of a clean and indoor life. Each of the cats has their own dishes in various areas of the house and just in case I forget where they are, Paige guides me to them at meal time. She is so helpful.

Simon is an orange ball of fur. He doesn't do much except purr when his mother is in the room. Not one to beg for table scraps he simply loves being in whatever room in our house Mother is in. Wherever she goes my wife is followed by a large orange plume. A simple pat on the head is all he asks for his devotion.

Chloe came to us from the SPCA. My wife asked for the feistiest feline in the room. Well, let me tell you something, we got it. She is affectionately known as the "Destroyer". I think I can safely say that nothing in our house does not had a paw print on it.

After putting the groceries away I must've left the receipt in one of the bags. It was her sole responsibility to take power over it. I have never seen paper shredded like that was. Exhausted from a firm thumping and tearing, the little tortoise shell found her self at nap-time on top of our rumbling dryer. What a Life!

Then enter Rozie, a sh'tsu. Since she lives with four cats, I think she thinks she is a cat too. I know she doesn't like any of the dogs in the neighborhood. Her job is to sit in the living room window and survey the street. She does a great job too. After all she weighs about twelve pounds. Her presence is known in our house. Our lives have been adjusted to revolve around her. It's our pleasure to do so. After returning from a family funeral I was certainly glad to be home among my treasures. Bette ignored me for leaving her, Paige was hungry, Chloe was involved in yet another adventure and Rozie was exhausted by the trip. Simon just sat and purred waiting for a pat on the head. Life is good.

Just a Pet

It was my wife who brought the black and white cat home. She had seen her run over on Prince Street and left for dead. It upset her terribly that people just drove around the obviously injured animal. "NO COMPASSION IN THIS TOWN" she shouted out in a letter to the paper. That caused a whole series of events that led to us taking this 'broken doll' home with us.

Paige is someone I felt never quite belonged to us. She was not one of our babies, she was a pet. For the next nine years she resided with us. She was not affectionate, well not really. She was very vocal. She made it known to us when she was hungry. Soft cat food please in the evenings, hard stuff throughout the day! Then I will enter a world of slumber and comfort in the basement of our house and as long as you two will have me, I will stay. But, and there's always a but, I am just a pet. I am not your personal property.

Paige is the one that stands out the most in our house. She photographs the best so it was always her photo that we showed off. The others girls like India and Bette may have been my personal babies but their photographs left a little to be desired. Her spirit shone through.

Paige was also never one to back down from a fight or to make her presence known unless it was to her liking. I am sure you all know what I mean. However, the nine years she spent with us were interesting just like she was and I grew to admire her. She was a great pet.

Where she ever came from was a mystery to us. Not something one likes to think about because what if the unthinkable happens, that someone discovers that we have her and they come to get her? Oh no, I thought to myself, we are definitely attached to her and her to us. Lay low, after all her life here is better than what we had imagined she came from.

Fate is fickle. Once, in a daring escape she wandered around for day or two. We placed Lost Cat posters and got many calls. To our surprise she found her way home to her original owners. They wondered where she had gone all those years ago and we wondered where she came from. Because of their kindness, Paige was able to come back home to us. They knew we had taken good care of her and why break up a happy home. Kind, right?

Paige is a genuine beauty. I tried on several occasions to tell her so and to show her how much I enjoyed having her join our family. I intended to convey to her that I wanted her to live out the rest of her days with us filled with comfort, good food and a warm bed. She would have no part of my adoration. Off to the basement. Every once in a while she would call out to me and I would be permitted to tickle her belly. Not for long and don't be too rough Buster! After all, this is all my idea and it must be executed on my terms or else. I am just a visitor here and you had better learn early on, that it will be done my way! Ok then.

Paige likes to eat, that's for sure. Turkey, pizza, bologna, cheese, all the things a house cat should never munch on. Too bad! She would tell you with her insistence. I want that stuff and I am relentless in my approach. Well then, since she is so street wise and tough, I guess it won't hurt her, will it? Nope!

Well, earlier this year she showed signs of slowing down. Getting old I told myself, these things happen. She can't eat like she used to. She's not really herself and what in the world is going to become of her? After all, she has been a terrific pet and we have to do right by her. Off to the vet only to find out the eating problem was due to a tumour that would eventually take her life. We had the option to put her down right there and then. Nope! Let's bring the resilient feline home; we'll know when it is time.

Time went by. Paige healed as best she could. Look for excessive drooling and mood changes, the vet told us. Well that's exactly what we witnessed. After a while, she was not eating like she should, she was getting weaker by the day and then the harsh realization that now might be the time we dreaded. So, what to do!

Today was the day. I took on the task at hand while my wife was at work. There in the quiet comfort of a dimly lit room, softly and gently, she left me. I stood there thinking about the last nine years and how they impacted us. She was just a pet, I thought to myself, or was she? Perhaps the tears on my keyboard may tell you a different story. Goodbye my precious girl, thanks for everything, I love you!

Just Plain Betty

Every once in a while I take inventory of my life and most times I walk away grateful. My mother taught me at an early age to be grateful for what you have, not what you do not have. Sound like great advice, right?

This is what I have today. My wife Sherry, my dog Rozie, and the home we all share. I also have the privilege of residing with the most dramatic cat actress, Bette Davis. Most people pronounce it "Bett" but really it's just plain Betty.

Plain might be the word to describe her. She tan in colour, with light green eyes. Oh those eyes, they were blinking at me this morning from the comfort of our day bed in the sun room. This very yellow room absorbs the morning sun in such a way that it makes it probably the most peaceful room in our house. At least my sleeping lamb, Bette thinks it does.

This is where Bette has chosen to spend most of her day. Since she is an indoor cat she has mastered the art of relaxing. I am sure that over the years I have learned the true meaning of comfort from that cat. Sunbeams are an asset to a perfect afternoon nap. Fresh water please, in the bowl would be nice but if I have to, I will drink it from the dripping faucet. Also, feed me please when my belly is hungry, I'll let you know when. Along with all of this, I want to reserve the privilege of walking on you at any time, snuggling into your neck early in the mornings, follow you around if I so desire and ignore you completely if that suits me. Are you cool with this entire situation Daddy? Yes Dear, I am.

I know you love me, she says with those eyes, the famous Bette Davis eyes. Those same eyes that reeled in the movies goers for decades now call the attention of the only man in this girl's life, Daddy. Now you know, in the cat kingdom, there is no relation ship between a male and the kittens. Mother does all the work. But in this case, because it suits her, Daddy is the one who carries her when she needs to be carried, protects her from the others when she has been bullied and loves her, just because.

Bette Davis does not meow. She doesn't have to. If she makes any kind of sound I come running. I guess a better way to put it is 'if she speaks, I listen'. Once, I heard a mournful cry from behind the couch. It seems she had her claw caught in the fabric and couldn't get free. She made her presence known and Daddy came to the rescue. In doing so I wanted to hug her and soothe her, she simply would have none of that. Bye, off she scampered to another room.

Some might say so but I assure you that Bette Davis is not a vain cat. She is simply the Queen of our household. She dominates the upstairs and is not afraid to put the run to the other cats that live in our house, is she so desires. Bette has had her portrait done by Robb Scott but she doesn't care about a picture. Why would you stare at that when you have the real thing in the room? I suppose.

So, it was November of '97 when I brought her home under my shirt. It was inevitable that she and I be together from the moment our eyes met. Okay, she was a little resistant but I managed to win her over. Over the years she has found comfort in my arms, on my chest, around my neck and in my heart. Will she live forever? No. Will I cry when she goes, you bet! I cry now if I think about it too much. However, there is always today and that brings me to that word again, grateful. Sherry is off to Halifax and I have the day to myself. It's hot today so any lounging today will probably be done in the living room where the air conditioner is. And after lunch, maybe we'll take a nap on the bed. Daddy, Rozie the dog and my lovely, my beautiful, just plain Betty! Life is good.

Within my Heart

People in general make assumptions based on their own life experiences and quite often are correct. In other cases they might be well off base. Why don't you decide for yourself...

Since my wife and I have no children of our own it has been assumed by those who do, that our pets have become our children. We have been accused of spoiling them beyond repair and due to something lacking in our lives, accept them as a decent replacement for kids. Perhaps they are right in such assumptions but allow me to explain myself. I love my dog! Let me say it again, I love my dog! She, Rozie is a comical, entertaining clown who worships the very ground I walk on. For the past few years she sits patiently waiting for me to come home from work everyday and gives me such a warm reception when I get here, that I quite often find myself hurrying home just to be near her. She sits at my feet, sleeps in my bed at my feet, takes me for walks, shares my snacks and loves me to pieces. Who, in their right mind could not love that?

There is something about a boy and his dog. At 40 years of age, I am about the biggest boy you will ever meet. I simply refuse to grow up and my dog will attest to that. She fills my heart with joy and love and makes me want to go to any length to protect her. I am smart enough to know that she won't be here forever but I also realize that these days we share are the important ones. Yesterday, a beautiful Nova Scotia summer afternoon, warm and sunny, I sat on my patio deck in a yard that my wife has painstakingly transformed into a flowery haven. We ate a marvellous summer meal and watched the dog chase a butterfly around the back yard. I couldn't help but appreciate my life. My wife and I both work, we have vehicles, a decent home that will someday be paid for and we have a dog. These are the days that fill my heart with love.

On the inside of our modest home we have four house-cats. They are my pets. Each one has their own personality, funny quirks and tastes. Some have some not so funny quirks and poor taste. However! On the wall in our living room hangs a framed black & white portrait of my cat India, a pitch black, green eyed vixen of amazing strength and determination. That girl, was not my pet for fourteen years, she was my daughter. I had never had a closer relationship with anyone, animal or not, than I did with that girl. She didn't sit at the top of the stairs barking and waging her tail when I came home. She didn't take me for walks or even chase butterflies. She simply owned me and that was that. She sat with me if it suited her, she slept in the bed with me if that was to her liking, not at my feet, on my chest. That was her place and she had sole rights to it. She was a determined and willful cat and I think that gave her the will to live to the ripe old age of fourteen despite the fact that she was diagnosed with feline leukaemia at the age of four. She opened my eyes to the beauty that is all around me and made me appreciate the color black. She also made me aware that things don't last forever. It is a hard lesson to learn but a realistic one.

It's been a year since India left me and not a day goes by that she doesn't cross this heart of mine. To tell you truth, I wish she didn't. I could use the break. The last year has been like every other one, I go through the motions, I go to work, I eat my dinner, I walk my dog. All in all I think I handled the whole situation well. I do appreciate my life and all it offers......but......... every once in a while I glance up into that portrait and there within the walls of my heart, she sits quietly and without harm. A pet, oh no people, that's my daughter.

How Much is that Doggie in the Window?

In an effort to make my dog's life as comfortable as possible I spoke to my wife about putting in a window seat so that the little dog, a sh'tzu, could have something to keep her occupied while we were at work.. She loved looking out the window from the end of the chesterfield, surveying her neighbourhood. She would do this for hours quite often falling asleep.

Building a window seat is no problem for my wife as she is very handy around the house. More so than I am. But it would also mean a disturbance to our living quarters. My wife and I and our dog are not the only ones who live in our house. We share our home with five indoor house-cats. Their ages range from twelve months to twelve years. Each comes with their own funny quirks and some even come with some not so funny quirks. That folks is another story. Still, my wife and I came up with a suitable solution by re-building a coffee table with a secure position beneath the window, complete with a soft pillow some five times the dog's size. What a life!

My dog Rozie is very special to the two of us. She is our first and probably our only dog. She has a great playful personality and loves to show it off. She knows her place in our home and she keeps my wife and I in line. It was my wife who insisted on getting a dog, I never wanted one. Too much work I thought to myself and besides, we both work. Still, we got one. My diligent wife crate trained the dog at first and made sure all her needs were taken care of, no matter what time of day or night. I couldn't help myself; I thought she was pretty cute. What I didn't know was that the dog had eyes for me. Although Mother was the one who took care of her, it was my arrival each day that the young dog anticipated. Anticipated with such warmth and love, I couldn't help but return the feelings. Soon, I was hooked. This was now, and will always be, my baby girl.

There's a price to pay for love. Every morning at six my little alarm clock wakes me up. "Come on Daddy! It's time to run up the road." While Daddy doesn't always feel like it, I had to realize that these things just have to be done. To tell the truth, if you knew what a selfish person I am, no one would ever think I would take the time 365 mornings a year to take care of business with that little dog. But, I have a responsibility to face. So, onward and upward we go. We've braved the cold, the snow, winds and rain and that was just yesterday.

On the freezing days Rozie doesn't want to step outside let alone the trek up the road, so we tried to do our business in the back yard. It doesn't work! So, like a big monster I force her to face the elements, telling myself that she is an animal after all, and that the two of us can make it. Then come the dramatics. If her paw is cold or frozen she lifts it in an effort to shield it from the weather and then she whimpers softly which pulls on my heart strings. "Okay then " I think to myself. "Today you can poop in the house."

"Okay, wait a minute, no that's not okay. She's a dog and I am a man. I am the one who should be whimpering. She's a dog, for heaven's sake, they poop out side, that's what dogs do!" "Let's get this over with and I'll take you back home and you can lie in the warmth of a sunbeam shining in our living room window, and relax on a window seat that Mother fashioned, and watch the whole world go by, while the two of us are out working so that we can provide you with such a lavish life. Cool?

Also, for what it's worth, other dogs don't live like this". I might as well be talking to the wall.

I honestly wonder if she's worth all this. And then something happens. After an exhausting day of neighbourhood watching, rounding up cats, greeting guests, sleeping in a sunbeam, eating a healthy supper and taking an evening walk, she cuddles up to her Daddy with sleepy eyes. Uh, oh, there's that face and that love I was talking about. My little girl, my baby dog. She needs me; she loves me, and just when I needed to be appreciated. So I had better get some rest. After all, tomorrow is another day.

So I ask, "How much is that Doggie in the window? Why, she's worth everything to me.

My Heart Will Go On

When you lose someone you love, it is such a deep pain that it leaves an indelible mark on your heart and soul. You do the best you can to accept the fact that this person is gone and that you really have to pick up and carry on. As hard as it is to do, it must be done, I should know. But, when you lose a pet that you are particularly fond of, the pain is a little more personal. This too I am fully aware of.

India was more than a pet to me, she was my buddy. Had she been a butterfly, a horse or an alligator, I still would have fallen in love with her if she showed the same spunk, determination and resilience. India gained my respect and that made me love her, but what definitely cemented our relationship was the fact that she chose to love me and place me above all others in her life. For that I was truly honored. Get what I mean?

She waited for me every day, sat with me while I watched television, lounged with me during the evenings and slept in my bed at night. I believe she saw me as her partner, her protector, her peer and her Daddy. For fourteen years the life she lived was one of comfort and I was happy to provide such comfort. I did right by her and she by me. No regrets right? No more pets either! My heart can't take it.

Oh, don't get me wrong, I love my dog and I love the other cats that live in my home. Robbie the Recluse, Paige the Broken Doll, Simon the Pretty Boy Kitty Boy, Chloe the Destroyer and Bette Davis, the most dramatic cat actress in the world. Sounds like quite a bunch, eh? Each comes with their own personalities and funny quirks, but I swear I will never get attached to any of them in that way. Still, it is Miss Bette Davis that has insinuated herself into my life and into my heart.

When she arrived she certainly made an impact. At that time this little kitten was a fireball that livened up the older cats. Not India! She hated everyone! But, and there's always a but, she tolerated Bette. That statement is saying a lot. At our house, it seems that India rules. She ruled with an iron fist not unlike Margaret Thatcher ran the British Isles, and believe me, no one dared to get in her way. In return she never mingled with the others, keeping much to herself, making the most of sunbeams, snoozing between two pillows in the bedroom, or surveying the neighborhood from any upstairs window of her choosing. When she ate her lunch no one dared move in and take some, hence the consequences.

Bette admired her from afar. She too would love to have snuggled in between the pillows but she could only do it when the Queen was out of the room. I think she would have loved to converse with India on many world topics but this all had to be done from afar. So be it. Still, when India passed away it left an open and empty spot in my life.

Now, quietly in the late evenings Bette softly makes her way into our bedroom, past the dog, walks over my wife and finds a comfortable spot on the blanket near my chest or shoulder. At four in the morning when the moonbeams shine brightly over our neighborhood, I am able to glance down there and see the tender soul who reaches out to me. There in the quiet of the moment, my heart fills to the top with love for this little vixen that too will someday leave me. Still, I think if all I have to do to make her life complete is to offer a shoulder, and then I feel it's my duty. My heart will give, my heart will hurt, my heart will heal and hopefully my heart will go on and on until one day when I cross over and find myself at a place called Rainbow Bridge where my heart will come full circle. Then I will know that my life was truly worthwhile.

This Story Has No Happy Ending

Iwarn you now this story has no happy ending. When my very black cat India died after living with me for fourteen years, I was heartbroken. The following year was torture for me because she wasn't just a pet, she was my little girl. Loss of a loved one, of any kind is painful and the best advice I can offer is to look forward and to get on with your life. Great advice, huh?

In an effort to end my grief my wife shocked me by bringing home a kitten for my birthday. I honestly could have killed her, my wife I mean, not the kitten. I not only did not want another pet, I absolutely didn't want anything to remind me of exactly what I had lost. I truly wanted to be alone in my grief. Grieving is nothing new to me. I lost my father at an early age, my grandparents, friends, my mother and now my little girl. I knew that time would take care of me and besides, I have a dog. But, my wife, God Bless her, thought this wild and crazy (which she calls feisty) tortoise shell cat would fill the void.

At first I couldn't stand the sight of her. There she was all different colors blended into a dark coat and a yellow patch over one eye. I couldn't even see her face clearly. Sherry called her Chloe and I called her Butterscotch Face. She was constantly disrupting the older cats, running and jumping about and crashing into things. Not the brightest little thing, I thought to myself. Always running from food dish to food dish diving in and helping herself to the other cats dinners. Much to their dismay I might add. And she was clumsy too! Continually knocking things over and smashing most that she touched, all I could think of was why would someone do this to me? I know my wife meant well but, hullo? It is quite possible that not one thing in our house has not had a paw print on it.

As the year progressed, Chloe, the wildcat grew to be larger than all the other house-cats and despite her juvenile approach to life she was fast becoming one of the pack. I thought for sure they all hated her but..... I don't know yet why the long established cat family in our home would allow her to join the group but they did. Robbie, my reclusive cat warmed up to her the most. This was something I never expected but then again I am constantly amazed by the animal kingdom, whether they are domestic or wild. Maybe as the oldest of our cats he was amused by the tireless, and I mean tireless energy of this youngster.

Then one day it happened, she went too far, she knocked the Christmas tree down. I was furious, my wife was upset but still she found it entertaining. Entertaining? You've got to be kidding; I was adamant that this crazy feline was to go. I want to tell you that I have never turned away an animal and for me to even say this was really shocking to all involved. But my wife stood strong and I of course, backed down. I guess I could learn to live with her, I am sure the crazy nut would outgrow the behavior and even the vet promised after Chloe was spayed that on or around 18 months she would calm down. Ha!

Anyway, as these stories go, I had a change of heart brought on by a choking noise in the middle of the night. I sprang from my bed toward a gasping and crying kitten that had gotten herself into something she shouldn't have. After a few quick moves on my part, I held in my arms what I had forgotten. I had been empty. This was a baby and I was her daddy. My heart was melting and I was able to look at her differently. I instantly learned to love that multi colored face. Will she ever take the place of my India? Nope! Chloe has made a place of her own. So onward and upward we go!

Oh Yeah, I lied about the happy ending, sorry!

Winter Meeting

Our pastures were lightly covered with snow. That is always a good thing. It's December and this is the time for snow. Since global warming is upon us, I feel much better when we have seasonal and predictable weather when we are supposed to. It's easier on my pets too. The horses consume hay and are happy to be in the warmth of the barns. I enjoy the walk to the barns in the morning. So does my dog, Rozay. She is a collie mix and is the most faithful companion a man could ask for.

Moving to a farm was the smartest thing my wife and I have ever done. The horses aren't ours. We allow the neighbor to use the facilities at his own risk. I much prefer chickens and ducks, and the wild deer that feed on the perimeter of our property. I built the henhouse myself; I even assisted in building suitable quarters for our ducks alongside the pond in our back yard. It really makes it beautiful. As winter settles in the chickens stay inside and get plump. Not only do they supply us with fresh eggs but they are sometimes, our main course. I cannot kill a chicken myself and I refuse to eat duck. I am too tender-hearted to do the killing but I do enjoy eating part. That goes for the beef too. My neighbor John Morgan always fills our freezer with freshly cut roasts and we enjoy them thoroughly.

The reason I live on a farm is to lower my stress level. It was either that or die, my doctor informed me. So I listened. I love chickens and view them more as pets than I do a farm animal. I just want them taken care of. The ducks are for a selfish reason. I fell in love with waterfowl as a boy and since then, I simply enjoy watching them and listening to them chat the day away. They are in their own little world and I do my best to keep them safe from any predators.

Up behind the barns, my wife and I each have a garden. In the summer months I grow vegetables and she grows flowers. Both are beautiful and cultivated. Mine is fenced in so the wild deer and jack rabbits don't eat all I've grown, and she has carefully crafted a fence for all her colorful and pretty flowers to embrace.

After working in business for so long I didn't think I would like all the quiet but I have adapted nicely. The air is clean and fresh and so is our life out here. It's the walks I take around the wooded property that fascinates me the most. To see wildlife in it's natural habitat in whatever form, is heartwarming.

There is a tall, old, wooden fence that separates our acreage from our neighbors, and it stands strong. All along the fence the view is beautiful. Quite often in the spring you will see a doe or two with a fawn. I thought the fence was to divide our properties, but later, I find out it was to keep the deer at a respectful distance. They really are beautiful creatures and as long as I knew the boundaries, I was able to view them without threat of interference on my part.

One doe in particular caught the scent of mine in the wind and that will usually cause the group to disperse. She seemed comfortable in my presence. Perhaps she had contact with man on a friendly basis over the course of time and felt un-threatened. I probably shouldn't do it but I often find myself bring carrot greens and apples to the fence and with my strongest arm, throwing them over. I know the deer enjoys this because I think they look for me. My newest friend, Sophie, moves the closest to the fence. She is like the lookout. Once she says it's okay, then it's a go for the rest.

There is something special about Sophie. She's gentler than the others and more trusting too. This could be a dangerous thing for all of us. That's why I try to keep a respectful distance. She does come close enough that I can see how pretty her eyes are. Eyes are the mirror to the soul, isn't that what they say? She looks at me tenderly and sometimes tilts her head in amazement, the whole time on the alert for noises in front and back of her.

Yesterday she didn't show. In fact none of them walked along the fence wall. It was a reasonable day and for the life of me, I could not imagine what was going on. After a day or two, things began to get back to normal. When I mentioned to John Morgan the mysterious events, he told me one of them must've given birth, and without Sophie, none would be allowed to leave the herd. All would form a circle around the doe and fawn until it was up and running. How magnificent, I thought this was a real miracle. John Morgan was right. There in the middle of the herd, a young doe had her fawn ever so near. Sophie, for the first time approached the fence. Standing inches from me, I could see her breath in the cool morning air, and had the chance to look into those beautiful eyes. From my hand I offered her a large carrot with a huge green top. Gently she took it from me and walked over and placed it at the feet of the young mother.

My heart was pounding so loud I could hear it in my ears. She really was the matriarch of the group. I think this little fawn was her grand-daughter and she brought them out to see me. I was never so humble in business as I was in the beauty of my own back yard.

Nature is wondrous, life is beautiful.

As the Crow Flies

My backyard is a veritable playground for birds and small wildlife. One never knows what they will see when you look out my kitchen window. Wild partridges are abundant at this time of year. The neighborhood cat usually frightens them off. Then there's the sparrows, the starlings, beautiful blue jays, wild canaries, you name it. Most of them take advantage of our trickling pond and all it has to offer. It must be fascinating as our cat never leaves the window, she enjoys the show.

Once in a while a deer or two will wander through our property looking for fallen apples. But it is a squirrel that has made it's home in the neighbor's barn that fascinates me the most. What a busy little guy he is scampering about our yard, gathering scraps of food that he can store to get him through the long winter. That's one thing man and animal have in common; we are all trying to weather the weather.

Last Sunday during a routine clean up in the kitchen there was a bag of unused home-made bit & bites that would not likely be of any use to anyone. So, I thought the birds might like it and they tend to make the best of anything at this time of year. It cannot be easy for them...

So, I use my best arm to hurl handfuls of this rather tasty snack as far up the hill as I can. If it's too close to the house it may go unnoticed so I did my best to get it into the clearing. Not a bird in sight. Well, I thought to myself, it'll take a little time but someone will discover it. Well, not too long afterward, the little squirrel came gliding down the hills of white and JACKPOT! Pine nuts and peanuts and hickory sticks and pretzels and cheezies, what more could a hungry soul ask for? The first thing he did was taste a cheezie, it must've tasted good because he grabbed the next one in his cheeks and up the hill he went straight to his home in the barn. Back and forth the little prince scampered filling his cheeks and returning to his nest.

Before long a bird or two noticed the orange dots in the snow and swooped down for a treat. First a mourning dove who cooed at the very sight of the feast and then let it known to her friends what was upon them. Then a blue jay, these birds are famous for chasing all others away but this guy wasn't true to form. He kept a respectful distance from the others. All is well.

Then, as fate would have it, the neighbor's cat spotted the clutch of fowl and did his best to make his way down the snowy hill through the crunchy stuff, of course, giving himself away. Off they flew, no massacre here thank goodness. I guess cats don't care for bits & bites so he didn't stick around for long. The feast resumed.

But as the crow flies it is usually a warning to all. Danger is near. These birds are big as chickens, the menace of the sky, terrorize the neighborhood, tear open garbage bags, threaten the existence of all those who live around them. No wonder Alfred Hitchcock chose the likes of them to terrorize movie audiences. I think they would love to have feasted on a little squirrel gumbo and probably would have had they not noticed the strewn about treats. So as fate would have it, the rest of this food was cleaned up by these massive scavengers leaving nothing but a hint of orange dust on the crusty snow. But I will tell you one thing, there's one fat and happy little squirrel in a cozy barn up the hill.

The Wind in the Trees

The wind in the trees behind our house kept waking me up. I am the type that needs his sleep. That's why I go to bed early so I can wake up and face the day ahead without being tired. Today was not a day like that. I was grouchy in the morning. Every time someone said good morning to me, I felt like punching them in the head. Every person that smiled at me, I wanted to throw something at them. Then my day got worse.

There was a detour on our snow covered road. I knew of a side road, although not paved, that would get me home and into my bed where I belonged. Again with the wind, this time it brought drifting snow. I kept going, knowing I was closer than not to home, so if I kept on the path I would get there eventually. I might be wrong though. As I look out my snow covered windshield I don't see familiar territory. Where can I be? I thought to myself. I didn't cross the river and so I must still be driving along side of it but there's no guard rail. Wow, this is different. I'm not slipping or sliding in the snow and I can't see through it very well but I don't seem to be in any danger. It's as if I am being guided along. Sorry but I don't have time for this. I have to get home.

That when I saw the smoke from the chimney up the road. I didn't even think anybody lived out here this far. Into the lane I pulled my car and got out. Again, the whistle of the wind in the trees. Lost in the woods in the middle of a snowstorm and I find this haven. It had better not belong to an axe murderer, I kept thinking to myself. No sign of life as I approached the humble camp. I could see the welcoming smoke from the chimney and the defined smell of burning wood. No tracks in the snow so whoever's here is inside. I knocked on the door, pounded really. The door opened and there before stood a tiny old woman with a shawl over her shoulders to keep warm.."Come on in" she said "you must be freezing," I have to tell you I didn't expect that. I either expected to see Grizzly Adams or the Hermit of Gully Lake, but I never expected Grandma Moses.

"I've got some tea on the stove, if you like." She smiled and said. The whole place, although tiny, was warm and welcoming. "What in the world are you doing way out here in weather like this?" she inquired. I might ask you the same thing, I though to myself.

"I guess I got off the beaten path" I told her innocently. I never bothered to mention that I was impatient and over tired and cranky. All of that didn't seem to matter anymore. I felt enormously at home in her presence. "Where are you from?" she inquired. I should've been more polite but I interrupted her and asked "Where exactly am I and why would someone of your advanced years live out here alone, so far from civilization, in this kind of weather?"

"I made a conscious choice after my husband died. I spend my summers at the shore and my winters here. Once a month a friend drops off supplies and I keep myself busy chopping wood and working around the place. I have my dog Hobo for company" I looked around and saw no dog. "He's out for a run" she informed me, "He'll be back soon and he'll give you a good going over." she laughed. Right on cue I heard a dog's bark outside. Expecting a Husky I must say I was surprised to see a black lab and a friendly one at that. Hobo greeted me like a was a member of the family. I felt relaxed for the first time in a long time.

"The sun will go down soon" she stated with expertise. "I fixed up a place near the fire where you can sleep. The weather will let up tomorrow and you'll be able to get away." "Thanks' I said, "For everything." Supper was beans and bread with more hot tea. I had a good night's sleep like I haven't had in years. I woke up at dawn feeling ten years younger. I took the time to thank Sara for her hospitality, Hobo too, and dug my car out and away I went.

Driving down the thin road was easy, again as if guided. That's when I spotted the Mounties car coming toward me. Driving slowly toward me, he flagged me over. "Hello there!" I said as I rolled down the window. "We thought you were a gonner" the older gentleman stated. "In this weather and so close to the river, we figured we'd be draggin' a body from the water, instead luck must've been with you."

Huh?

"When I got the call that a car was stuck in the snow and ice on top of the river I figured it would have sunk before we could get to it but you stayed afloat. You must've passed out from the cold". Passed out? I thought to myself. "Not quite, I had an interesting night. I spent it in a warm cabin at the end of the lane. The nice lady served me beans and hot tea". The cool wind whistled around my car. He looked puzzled "Hasn't anybody lived up here in fifty years. Last one was my mother and her dog Hobo. She died rescuing her dog right here on this river."

I never spoke a word.

As I pulled into my driveway and got out of my car, I felt a gust of wind through the trees. It was filled with the aroma and fragrance of baked beans and steeped tea. Sara was with me, Hobo too. They were my guardian angels.

Four Cats of Prince Street by Richard Todd Canton

One cannot co-exist in a world with members of the animal kingdom without being inspired by them. I found my pets to be both entertaining and intelligent. So what's a guy to do. I animated them and put them into a series of adventures for the young at heart. I introduce you to the Four Cats of Prince Street thru a young kitten's eyes and how big the world seemed to her even though she has never been on the other side of the door:

A Hero Among Us
The story begins....

The panicked, slender beige and white cat raced down the hall and under the day bed. Who's that?" asked Bette. "He sure looks scared". "He is!" replied Rory. "His name is Robbie, and he is better off left alone. He never bothers with anyone." Bette watched intently as Robbie quickly slipped out of sight into the privacy under the day bed in the den. Once she had looked under there. It was cluttered and full, a great place to snoop but she would never want to spend a lot of time in there. Out here there is so much more to look at and rummage through. Everyday is a new adventure. Still, Bette was curious about the stranger. He certainly was visible when it was feeding time. Then he was brave. But soon as that was over back he would go into the mysterious other world under the day bed.

The thing that a curious cat like Bette enjoyed the most about her new home on Prince Street was that there always was something new to discover. Rory was fast becoming her best friend. She remembers the first day Daddy brought her home. It was Rory who greeted her at the top of the stairs. And what a big lion he was. He was orange from head to toe. He possessed a large mane. Often times when Bette tried to look into his face she would topple over backwards. Rory was so massive and fierce looking, yet gentle at the same time. She soon learned the ropes and a lot of life's lessons from this great king. He was, after all the oldest and wisest of all of the cats at Prince Street.

With this great wisdom and experience there came a sense of responsibility. A great responsibility that he took seriously. It was his duty to protect the kingdom, to teach new members respect and to oversee all that went on while Mother and Father were gone for the day.

Routine is necessary to cats. They like to live a predictable and comfortable life and expect to enjoy the luxuries afforded them. Meals are served at specific times and all parties have become accustomed to their daily rituals. Six AM, Twelve noon, and Six PM sharp! It is Mother whom they all adore. She is 'the food lady'. She can perform magic. Mother is able to do things that cats can only dream about, she can open the pantry door, that is where the food is. Mother is able to do this with one hand. Rory cannot perform the task with his two. Mother can open the drawers and take out a fantastic piece of equipment, one that is idolized by pets everywhere; the can opener. Many times Rory has wished that he, the king of beasts, could only have been given the power and privilege to be able to operate the can opener. Such is the stuff dreams are made of.

The penthouse is a spacious one. The rooms are large and beautiful. It is easy to see that those who are chosen to live there do so in great style and comfort. There is not one place to sleep, rather a half a dozen. The feline bathroom does not contain one toilet but three. There are carpets to roll on, shiny waxed floors to slide on, a bathtub to hide under, and a refrigerator tall enough that when you sit on top of it you are able to get a clear view of your kingdom. Bette felt at home from the very beginning. She liked the people who adopted her, and she liked where they lived. The sofa was comfortable, the bed was even better.

But upon entering the bedroom one must face two very deadly enemies. First, the Queen; India von halkien, an elegant and exotic beauty. Bette was able to notice at first glance how beautiful she was. Rich black fur, and piercing emerald eyes. A shiver went down Bette's spine at the mere sight of the Queen she had only ever heard about from Rory.

High up on top of the bed, India peered over the side and looked down upon the newest member of this elite club. She appeared unimpressed. She knew what her task was. This little one must learn that there are some things that you do not do, and bothering the Queen is one of them. She arched her back, widened her tail and pounced with such power and strength that the only recourse Bette had was to flee. And she did! India was then able to resume her position smiling to herself, confident that she had successfully made her point. She knew that Bette was not going to be a problem.

The second enemy sneaks up on you. It roars its way up the hall and into the room you are occupying. It comes right at you with no fear. All you can feel is sheer terror. If you are able to find cover, it will roar past you, back and forth, sucking up everything in its path. The vacuum. Loud and overbearing, it is truly the enemy. Bette learned this the first day when even Rory ran from it. This too was a daily ritual and one had to prepare for its arrival. Bette first sought from refuge from it under the chair in the den and then into Robbie's private world under the day bed. She sat shivering while the nasty vacuum did it's work. Her nerves were nearly shot, she was crying and all she wanted was to go far away.

Robbie was able to see the terror on the little girl's face. He sympathized with her. In his own way he tried to comfort her. Nothing seemed to work. It was then that he decided to show her a trick he had learned. Leaving her in the safety of his hideout he looked outside, the coast was clear. The vacuum was far down the hall past the kitchen. Robbie flew like a flash around the corner down the hall into the bedroom. There it was, the extension cord that gave the vacuum life was plugged into the wall socket. Quickly, swiftly he ran towards and with the strength of ten men pulled the plug. The vacuum was dead. There was silence.

Mother hollered from down the hall. "Oh Darn! What is wrong with this vacuum cleaner?" She stomped up the hall to the bedroom. She could see the plug pulled from the cord, and felt confused. In her mind she wondered how this happened. She accepted that perhaps they had all had enough. She put the vacuum away.

Back underneath the day bed Robbie looked into Bette's eyes. He said nothing. He didn't have to. His actions spoke for themselves. She had found a brave new friend. She nodded to him as she was leaving the room. He nodded back. When she told Rory what Robbie had done and how brave she thought he was Rory explained that there was a lesson in life to be learned here. Robbie the Recluse was who he was for a reason. Long ago illness caused him to be deaf. He survives the best he can in this world without the acute hearing required by cats. He relies on his other instincts for survival. "When he saw how scared you were, he took it upon himself to show you that despite all your fears you can persevere. Sure the vacuum would be back the next day, but as each day approaches you may get a little braver." "So little one, respect Robbie's privacy and accept that there is a hero among us."

As Time Goes By
The Four Cats of Prince Street continues.....

"**Y**ou're not supposed to be up here in the attic." Rory's voice boomed. Bette turned around quickly and looked at him. "But it is so wonderful here and there is a lot to look at" Bette answered. Bette is such a curious cat that Rory knew it would only be a matter of time before she discovered the attic and all its treasures. One storage box was open and Bette had been able to squeeze herself inside. She showed Rory what she had found. It was a framed picture of a cat, the same cat whose picture is on the wall in the living room. When Mommy is dusting, she always pauses for a moment and stares at that picture.

A tear came to Rory's eye as he looked at the picture. A flood of memories came rushing back. "Her name is Angel and she also had lived here at Prince Street, but that was a long time ago." As Rory studied the photograph, he was able to see Angel as though she were standing there with him once again. "She was the most beautiful tigress I have ever seen. She looked a lot like you but with a darker tone to her coat. Her eyes were sea green and full of life and she was someone else that Daddy had brought home but not from a pet store or from a pampered home. Daddy rescued Angel from a rooftop on Queen Street. When she came to us, the poor girl was dirty, tired, and hungry.

Not all cats live like we do little one. Some are taken home as kittens and are treated royally but when they get older they are often tossed aside and usually find themselves out in the cold. It's a tough old world out there for a cat on the street, some make it and some don't. Angel was street smart and tough and she was a survivor. I remember the day that Daddy and Mommy brought her home. It was just me and India then. No one ever thought that there would be room for another. Angel was full of life and was so happy to have finally found a home. She had been bounced around a lot. At first it appeared difficult for her to accept that this was it, a real home, the one where she would finally find contentment, she was on the defensive and so was India. After all India had never seen another cat except for me and I don't even think she knew any others existed. She was a little taken aback by this brassy stranger.

Angel and I became friends almost immediately and as time went on the two girls got used to each other. Angel was shy at first but soon realized that there were no enemies here. She was sleeping in a warm bed, eating good food, was starting to feel happy, and was beginning to relax. Our main concern was to get her well and daily exercise became routine. Angel was feisty and full of vigor and we had fun chasing each other and wrestling. Even though she was half my size, Angel was able to hold her own when it came time for battle and she usually won. It was soon evident that Angel was becoming attached to me and me to her. I watched her grow and change and I watched how Mommy was also becoming attached to her. There is so much love in Mommy's heart and she loves us all in different ways. Daddy says Mommy loves all animals and that is why Angel came to live with us. Mommy cannot turn her back on anyone in need and she takes care of all of us.

Angel was away from us only once and that was because of an overnight trip to the vet. Since it is so important to be spayed or neutered, Angel too joined the ranks and her recovery was quick. When she came home from the vet, she was groggy and there was a tiny incision on her belly with a half a dozen stitches. Dr. Gwen told Mommy and Daddy that Angel was to take it easy for a few days so she would heal properly. But Angel, being such a feisty critter, was soon up and running, jumping, and playing. Over the next year Angel was able to realize that she finally had the family that she had longed for. Everyone was happy, even India, although she really didn't want to admit it.

Feline Leukemia is a cat killer. It is a disease that affects the immune system wearing down resistance until a cat is too weak to fight any longer. It can be transmitted from other cats through drinking water or sharing the same bathroom. Dr. Gwen said Angel probably picked it up, before we found her, from drinking out of dirty puddles or from another cat in the neighbourhood. She also said some cats can live a long time with the disease and others can go right away. Our Angel was fine at first. She recovered from her operation and was soon back in the race. It was a year or so later that Angel began to show signs of weakness. She started to lose energy and sometimes would go off to be by herself. While this made everybody worry, I don't think anybody realized that it would be the end.

For the last week of her life Angel spent most of her time on the daybed in the den. Quite often she would just stare out the window saying nothing. Angel's eyes were losing their sparkle and she was getting thin as it had become increasingly harder for her to eat. It was then that I realized as I looked through the doorway that this was someone that I truly loved. Daddy would hold her and talk to her, and she loved Daddy a lot. He was her hero and she was grateful that he was the one who insisted on bringing her home. But it was Mommy whose heart was breaking, she has only one family and that is us. This is why she gives us so much 'loves.'

It was late in May when Daddy left with Angel in the small blue cage. She was wrapped warmly in one of his tee-shirts. He wasn't gone that long but when he did come home it was with an empty cage. Our Angel was gone. That day Daddy didn't feel so brave, he was very sad. Mommy was mostly silent. Mommy tried very hard to be brave and on the outside she was, but inside she was very sad. She would still go to work every day and when she came home India and I would always greet her at the top of the stairs. Mommy always likes big 'loves' and this helped to heal her heart but I knew that nothing and no one could ever take the place of her Angel.

Bette had hung on Rory's every word. She had often wondered about the cat in the picture in the living room. Rory looked down into Bette's tiny face and smiled at her. "It is because of Angel that you are here, little one. She has helped to make a place for homeless cats like you and Robbie and has helped to prove that you really can make a space in your home and your heart." Bette thanked Rory for telling her about Angel and went downstairs to find Mommy. When she did, she purred and gave her big 'loves'.

What's the Matter with Rory?
The Four Cats of Prince Street continues......

India told Bette and Robbie to meet her in the den. She instructed them to sit down and listen. She spoke;

"I know that you both know that Rory has not been feeling well so all of us have to respect his state and act accordingly". Bette looked up into India's face and said, "You make it sound like he is going to die". A sad look came over India's face.

"Since no one is sure what's going on with him, the weight loss and his painful crying all the time, one never knows". Bette began to weep. Robbie did his best to console the little girl by saying. "Keep your hopes up, little one, after all Rory is the King. He has been down rough roads before and always made it through". Robbie looked away from Bette and although he was able to hide his pain from the little girl, his heart was hurting for his friend, his best friend, Rory, the gentle giant.

Mommy sat holding Rory and when Daddy entered the room she said to him. "We had better take him in because he isn't getting any better". Rory laid there in his weakened state with dull fur and watery eyes. India, Robbie and Bette watched as they carried the sick cat out the door. It is always a hopeful sign when they take any one of them to the Vet. Dr Gwen is such a kind and gentle doctor that it makes everyone feel better just knowing how much she cares.

As the three of them sat looking out the window as Mommy and Daddy drove away, India leaned in close to them. "We must all stick together, we are a family."

India settled down on the chesterfield for a little summer slumber but found herself restless and woke with an anxious shiver. There before her in haze of a summer afternoon appeared Angel. India quickly raised her head. "Angel is that you?" The vision did not speak. Yes, it was our Angel bringing a message. India's heart began to race. She sat up completely alert to the situation. What is it Angel trying to say? Is it Rory? Is he going to die? What is it? India looked around. Robbie and Bette were no where to be found. Again, she turned toward the vision. "What are you trying to tell me Angel?"

Angel softly spoke "I bring you Hope" and as quickly as she appeared, she faded into the air. A warm feeling ran over India's body. She knew it was all real and if God sent an Angel from heaven with a message then he must want us all to know that he lives and someday we all will join him. That is a good thing.

India didn't waste anytime telling Robbie and Bette the good news. All of them felt a great sense of relief. To them they knew Rory would be okay. All three sat and waited for Mommy and Daddy to return with their friend. However it was a shock to them all when the parents returned empty-handed. India assumed that Rory just had to stay overnight. Sometimes that happens. She knew that being empty-handed was a good thing because that means there was no cage, (empty or otherwise) so that meant that they had to go back.

Mommy spoke:

"Kids I have some bad news" "It's about Rory......

The words faded into the back of India's head as she glanced out the window into the world. To her shock and dismay she could see there in the back seat of the car, the small blue cage. It was empty. She knew this meant one thing. That Rory was gone. They would never bring the cage back empty. It always stays at the vet and comes home when the cat does. The last time they brought the cage home empty was when Angel had to be put to sleep.

India was beside herself with grief. She could not believe this was happening, not our Rory. All she could do was cry. India found refuge under the bed and there she stayed for the next two days. No coaxing from Daddy could get her out. Mommy tried and even Bette tried to persuade her but to no avail. In her sadness and grief India lost all hope. She could not even hear the words that were spoken to her. Nothing mattered anymore. Her thoughts were all about Rory and just how much she loved him. All she could do was cry.

Mommy was so confused about India's behaviour but she also knew how moody India was. She would come out when she was ready. In the meantime there was a lot to do. Mommy had to be educated as to treat diabetes. Rory's weight loss and constant thirst were sure signs that Rory had diabetes, a killer of cats. Dr Gwen did tell Mommy that if properly attended the diabetes could be kept under control and so Mommy set out to do just that. She had to learn about the blood-testing, injections, insulin, and syringes. Mommy was determined to save her boy. Later today she would go get Rory from the vet but not before Daddy fixed the handle on the small blue cage. That's why they brought it home.

You can imagine India's surprise when Mommy and Daddy brought home a ragged and tired Rory up the steps. She knew right then and there that she must continue to believe.....

Well it took a while to get Rory regulated but that is exactly what Mommy did. All the prodding and poking but Rory began to show signs of recovery and before long he was alive and well. They, the Four Cats of Prince Street we all together again. Rory, the Gentle Giant, India, the Queen, Robbie the Scaredy Cat and Baby Bette Davis.

There's Always Room For Hope
The Four Cats of Prince Street continues.....

You can imagine the surprise on everyone's face when Mommy came up the stairs and into the living room without saying a word. Whatever she was up to must have been important because she kept the door closed. This went on for days. Not an easy thing for cats to be kept from anything. We all know how curious they can be. India, especially was determined to get to the bottom of all of this. Bette was very curious as well because that was the room where she and Mommy would cuddle. Bette liked that and so did Mommy.

After a few days of this mystery they were allowed in, one by one. Rory who had quite often lingered outside the door knew that there was something in there. He could hear cries in the night coming from the other side of the door. He was quickly the first one in and took advantage of the opportunity. There was a bowl of water and then a poop pan and in a makeshift bed there it was.......and injured female cat. Rory thought she was pretty at first site, sleek and black and white with green eyes (his favourite). The injured cat was so groggy that all she could do was lie there. She could barely lift her head. "Rory, say hello to Hope. She's come to live with us for a while." Rory looked up into Mommy's face and back at the injured cat. She didn't look well at all.

Mommy went on to say;

I found her up the road. She had been run over by a car and whoever hit her didn't stop, they just kept driving. I would never leave her there. She was trying to crawl to safety but she was so badly hurt that she couldn't manipulate her body. Before I could get to her a man in a van pulled up and rescued her. He took her to the vet and I went and got her. You know me Rory, I cannot turn my back on any animal." Mommy was right about that! She loves the animal kingdom. She probably would bring home every animal if she could.

Rory was accepting, Bette was curious, as was Robbie but it was India's reaction that caught everyone off guard. India is never friendly to anyone new. India plays no favourites, she hates everyone equally. So all were surprised when she stepped up to the sickbed and leaned forward and whispered. "Hello Hope, I guess you were what Angel meant when she said she was sending Hope" There must be someone very special reason in order for you to have arrived in our home and into our lives. Welcome to Prince Street and all it has to offer. I know you will be happy here." India left the room.

All were curious as to who this stranger was. Of course there was hissing and growling at first but soon everybody was able to relax. Hope is the newest member of the Cats of Prince Street. We don't know how long she will be with us so we will all try to make the best of it.

We are all thankful that an Angel sent her to us. Always remember that Angels bring Hope and we are the proof. Paige Hope Canton is a black and white beauty that we often refer to as the Broken Doll.

A Lesson Learned
the Four Cats of Prince Street continues....

India, the Queen of Prince Street, was sound asleep at sunup. She was awakened by the stream of light that came in through the bedroom window and straight into her eyes. She was not amused. She wasn't ready to get up yet so she turned her back to the window and almost immediately she fell back to sleep. After all who would want to get out of such a comfortable bed anyway. It is a king-size bed and has four pillows, two puffs, clean sheets and is so fluffy and warm. Daddy was already up and in the bathroom shaving. India knew his routine as well as she knew her own. What time to bed and what time to rise. On those mornings when Daddy would forget and oversleep India knew what her duty was and that was to walk on him and to purr in his ear. He liked that. Especially on Saturday and Sunday mornings. He always told India "Oh thank you for waking me when I don't even have to get up!" You're welcome Daddy!

India assumed that today would be like every other day. Daddy would call her for breakfast and if she felt like it she would go down and take a look at the food and if she felt like eating she would and if she didn't she would promptly turn her nose up at it. This worries Daddy. Daddy has told her over and over that he only buys the best food for his girl. It costs over fifty dollars a bag but he says it's worth it because it is a special formula for cats with her condition. The same goes with the spring water that is served fresh every morning. She promised Daddy that she would eat her meals regularly to keep up her strength but today she forgot that deal. Besides she always enjoys it when Daddy picks up her dish of food and follows her down the hall and tries in a soft voice to persuade her to eat. Sometimes she does and sometimes she doesn't.

India is quite aware of how much she can get away with. After all it was Daddy that brought her home from the pet store. He told her that he would take care of her forever. Daddy has constantly pampered her and spoiled her and that is the way she likes it. He does get upset with her when she walks on the kitchen table or hounds him for his food. But she knows that he will always forgive her and let her have a treat of some kind. With that she knows that she is the winner. A winner is able to walk past her brothers and sister with her nose in the air right down the hall into the bedroom where she prefers to spend most of her time. She doesn't like going into the other rooms where everyone else hangs out. This also makes Daddy worry.

When Mommy comes home from work every night she too pays special attention to all her cats. Mommy is so nice and so beautiful. If you need your nails trimmed or your fur brushed she's the one to do it. She is also the food lady. She walks up to the pantry door and opens it and there it is; the large bucket with the scoop. By suppertime India is usually hungry as she doesn't always eat a lot for Daddy at noon.

That night after supper Rory was continuously bothering her so India looked forward to retiring early and she hoped her parents did too. Once they settle into the big bed she can always find a cosy spot for herself somewhere in there. They always close the door and those other kids; Rory, Robbie and Bette can't come in and bother us while we're sleeping. It is always so nice when the three of us are in there together.

One Friday Daddy had received a lot of phone calls. He and Mommy were called to the city and they said they would likely spend the night. India agreed but she didn't totally realize that she would be all alone for the evening. Daddy and Mommy were confident that everything would be okay. After supper that night they got into his car and drove away.

The evening was sultry. India just couldn't sleep. She tossed and turned and every once in a while she would get up and look out the window. From their bedroom high above the rest of the houses you could have a unique overview of the neighbourhood. Sometimes she would sit on the window sill and take a look up in the dark sky at the moon and stars. She enjoyed the breeze , although it was a small one, that came in the window. Again she tried to sleep, this time drifting off quickly. She was sound asleep when she heard the scratching noise. She new right away that it must be Rory. He must've come into her room since the door was left open and India was sure that he was just there to bother her. She heard the scratching noise again. This time it came from the window. She could see Rory's silhouette in the darkness. She called his name. He didn't answer. She asked him what he thought he was doing in this room, at this time, in that window. "I'm not Rory" he replied. India rose up to take a better look at the figure in the window. As she approached the stranger her heart began to pound with fright. "Who are you?" she demanded to know. "My name is Richard and I am hungry." His voice was deep and resonant. As she looked closer she could see that he was not a cat at all, instead he was a large racoon. The same racoon that she had noticed one other evening rummaging through the neighbor's garbage. She remembered thinking how disgusting she thought that it would be for someone to do that.

"You had better get away from that window right now Mister!" she ordered. "No one is allowed in here and when my Daddy comes home he will not be very happy to see you!" Richard looked around the spacious room and then back at her and grinned "Your Daddy won't be home tonight now will he?" India was shocked and surprised. She said nothing. She stood there frozen, staring at him, wondering how he knew, had he been there before?, what else does he know? She started to speak but he cut her off. "It would be wise for you to go to the kitchen quietly to get me some food and to bring it back here unnoticed. Do it and no one will get hurt." "But, how will you get the food? The window is locked, and there is a screen on it."she asked nervously. "You let me worry about that. Now do as I say." She left the room immediately and brought back a fistful of bread pieces that Mommy had broken apart for the birds. She started back down the hall. These should be small enough to push through the screen, she thought to herself. When she entered the bedroom there was no one in the window. He was gone. Well good enough she said to herself and turned to throw the bread crumbs out. She got the surprise of her life when she turned around and Richard was sitting on the floor right in front of her.

She immediately looked back at the window. It was then she noticed that the screen had been carefully removed. She turned back to face him. In the light reflecting from the hall she got a better look at him. His fur was not sparkling and shiny like her own and when she looked down she noticed that his right paw was covered with dried blood. "Are you okay?" she asked. His eyes looked tired. "Just give me the food before I faint" He held out his dirty paw. She looked down at her own well manicured paws. He immediately shoveled the food into his mouth and a look of satisfaction came over his face. It was then she knew that he probably had not eaten for quite some time.

"I have more food" she told him softly "if you're still hungry.""There is some good food in the pantry and if you help me we can get the door open and find it."He agreed and the two of them headed down the hall to the kitchen. Richard was able to turn the handle on the first try and soon he was delving into delicious and nutritious food. He ate until he was full. When he was finished he and India talked. She asked about his home and family. He explained to her that he was homeless. Humans had taken him home as a pet when he was a baby but when he got a little older and started getting into things, they set him loose.

Since he had no one to teach him how to survive in the wild he was left to wander the streets of Truro rooting through garbage and drinking water from puddles. He had not had a bath in a while and felt sick most of the time. Richard was forced to sleep in trees at night so larger predators roaming the neighbourhood would not catch and kill him. When they were through talking he quietly made his way down the hall and out the same window he came in. He turned to India and said softly 'thank you' and he was gone. It was at that moment that India realized the problem.

The next morning when Mommy and Daddy returned home, India was at the top of the steps with the rest of the family to greet them. She nuzzled her father especially well. "I guess that you missed me, eh girl?" "Well come on then it's time to feed everybody." They all went down the hall and India was first in line. When Daddy poured her food into her sparkling clean dish she gave him humongous loves. She ate all her food for him that day and for all the following ones. She now knew that she was truly blessed. India knew that she was a very fortunate cat.

Don't Go Near the Door

No one was quite sure how it happened but somehow the downstairs door got open and the baby got out. Rory knew that India would have to have had something to do with it. She was one of three who could open the door and he knew he didn't do it. Robbie never comes out from under the daybed so how did it happen? One thing was for sure. If she had indeed allowed Bette to venture outside, putting her at great risk, then there certainly were consequences.

Rory whispered at the mouth of Robbie's hideaway. ""We need you, the baby got out!" Robbie immediately popped his head out of his very private world, blinking at the light. "What?, How?, When? Rory told him "I'll explain it all later, but now we have to move" Robbie knew exactly what Rory meant. Time was of the essence. The two quickly strapped on their backpacks and up through the roof hatch they went.

The November winds were cold and rain had fallen steadily for days. Poor Bette cold and desperate became disoriented and soon found herself lost. Crouching near the cold bricks of the elementary school, Bette found a little shelter from the storm. She sat quietly waiting for Rory's voice to call her name. As the evening began to set in, she knew they would be worried about her. She knew Mother and Dad would not be home until morning and that Rory, her hero, would rescue her. All she had to do was sit and wait. Sit and wait was what she did. From pure exhaustion she passed out. This of course, was moments before Rory and Robbie made their way down Alice Street in search of the young kitten. The winds grew stronger and colder. Snow was in the air. Bette was cold and tired and hungry. Rory feared for her very life. All he could picture was how delicate she was as a kitten and what a close call they had then. She was his baby.

With all that was against them the weather, the wind and the night, it was all so hopeless. Rory and Robbie had to turn back. When they reached the stairs of Prince Street India was surprised that they turned up emptied handed. "I might as well explain what happened" she snapped at Rory. Rory's eyes were cold as steel as he fiercely glared a the snobbish black cat. "It's all her fault, continually pestering me as to what it was like outside. So when I finally had enough, I opened the door for her to take a look. That's when a gust of wind and rain came up and swept her up. I ordered her to come back in and that's when the wind blew the door shut. I couldn't get it open again, I tried, believe me"

India couldn't believe the coldness in Rory's voice. "It was our agreement that all who reside at Prince Street deserve the rights of passage. You have broken the rules and you know the consequences. If that child is not returned to Prince Street, and soon, you will be banished from Prince Street forever!" This really put India's nose out of joint. Down the stairs she stomped and opened the big door. She took a look out at the windy, rainy night and back upstairs at Rory. She had never seen him like this before. Robbie was cowering behind him like the coward she knew he was. One last look at the two and out the door she went with a big bang slamming behind her.

India lived a life of luxury, one she often took for granted, but this certainly was a wake up call. Her beautiful fur coat was drenched in the damp evening storm and this just made her all the madder. As she walked along Wood Street something drew her toward the school. In a moment of calmness she hear the familiar cry of the baby. She walked toward the sound just as the wind came up again. She found an even more drenched Bette Davis lying in a ball freezing. She guided her home and delivered her to Rory. She laid the drenched baby at Rory's feet and turned toward the door once more. She knew, more than most, that she was no longer welcome at Prince Street, so she left.

So unsure of where the night would take her she walked along the curb of the road. Up the hill she ventured until she saw the lights of an oncoming vehicle. Through the rain she could see the silhouette of another cat. The rain was falling heavy and that made the night all the less visible so of course the driver did not see it's impending victim. A loud thump sent the cat sprawling on the cold pavement ending face down in the water. The car drove on. India made her way across to the injured animal to see if there was anything she could do. As she got closer she realized it wasn't a cat at all, it was her racoon friend Richard, someone she never expected to ever see again. He started to lift his head, letting out a few groans. "It's okay Richard" she said gently stroking his back. "Who is it?" he inquired while a gush of blood ran down his head into his eyes. "It's me, India" Relieved, he said 'Oh, the Queen" "I'm hurt" his head fell to the ground. "Just get me home would you?" "I live a ways up the hill in the large Maple." India viewed Wood Street as a suddenly steep hill but she knew what she had to do.

Richard was nearly twice her size but that cat did everything she could to get him up that hill. It took a while and Richard was able to walk a bit of the way but for the most part she had to carry him. Determined, she reached the tree and subsequently pulled him up into the hollow of the maple where the bachelor racoon resided.

Despite the humble surroundings the tree home was cozy. India made Richard an elixir from sap and fed him small amounts while the ailing racoon drifted in and out of consciousness. By morning he was looking better. India knew nothing about nursing, she was always the one who required care, she never administered it. Today felt right. For once she was needed.

The next two days were spent with Richard convalescing. The winds had subsided and India was able to open a window to allow fresh air to breeze through the tree. She even cleaned up his place and made herself at home. Unaware as to how long she would be here, she accepted this as her own fate.

One morning she and Richard spoke about Victoria Park. It was long a dream of his to move there and begin a new life. He had been there once as a child but his life had taken a different path when he ventured to the wrong side of the tracks. His mother warned him that where the humans were was no life for a racoon. There was too many temptations out there for him but he did not heed his mother's advice. He, a rebel of racoons, travelled the rough road and was all but abandoned by his family.

After listening intently to his story, India insisted that there was no time like the present to begin living a dream. I guess because he had suffered such a close call, procrastination was no longer an option, the two set out on their journey.

Making their way through the thicket the two formed an unbreakable bond. She felt needed for the first time in her life and he felt a new zest for life. His coat seemed to get shinier and her's a little duller but still they trekked on, enjoying the moment in time. Talking, laughing and talking some more.

As sunrise the next morning arrived, they set out on the journey, Victoria Park was as beautiful as he remembered and even more stunning than India had ever imagined. It was truly a racoon's paradise. The river was full and the sound of the water flowing was relaxing and kind. The air was fresh, the trees beautiful and the warm sun was making it's way through the branches. No wonder animals and humans alike enjoyed all Victoria Park had to offer. As she stood there looking around and absorbing all the beauty, thoughts of home were creeping into her mind and weighing on her heart. She knew it time to go. She also knew Richard would be much better off here and would get along fine back amongst his own kind. She whispered to him that she felt it was her time to leave. "I cannot tell you how much you mean to me" he said tearfully. "I have never had a true friend before and I do not want to lose you" "I love you" she began to weep at the kind words. "I love you too......I really do". She turned to leave. Just as she was about to turn the corner she glanced over her shoulder to see Richard being welcomed by a racoon that looked amazingly like him. A brother or a cousin perhaps. Again she felt happy.

As she scampered down the hill toward home her heart was filled with love. Not just for Richard but for those she left behind. As she approached Prince Street, a nasty Tom jumped in her path. As he grinned at her with nasty smile, he assumed that she was easy prey for whatever he chose. Well, from the very pit of her existence she let a howl and a growl that would frizzle the mane of a wild beast. It scared the tom off. As she walked down the sidewalk she chuckled to herself "I've still got it!"

Slipping in the big door unnoticed, she could not hear a sound upstairs. Looking down at her tattered coat, she look less like a Queen than ever before but still she knew herself better than ever. She softly crept up the quiet stairs and into the kitchen. Rory stood at the window looking out and without turning around asked "Are you home to stay?" . "Yes" she answered solemnly. "If you will have me." At that moment a frisky Bette came flying down the hall laughing and playing. Rory turned and looked down at the tiny creature and smiled. She looked up and into India's face "Rory said you would be back, cause this is the place you belong, with the ones who love you." Bette went on her way. India's eyes began to fill up with tears. She turned to see that Rory was looking at her. "I am glad you decided to come home, home to those who love you........"

103

Time Marches On

It was upon the death of Rory Canton, the King of Prince Street, that India vonhalkien accepted the role as Queen of the Castle. There was no doubt in anybody's mind as to whom was in charge. She was the Queen long before the titled was ever imposed.

The days were long now and the March winds whistled around the rooftop. As India stared out the window as she often did, lost in thought, she would gaze up into the skies and reminisce about Rory and the life they led together for so long. A noise in the hall brought her back to reality. Robbie was out and about, and Bette who was by now, a young woman, was mourning the loss of her closest friend, Rory, the Gentle Giant. "Why do people have to die?" She asked with a child-like innocence. India was quick to sternly answer "We all have to go sooner or later and my advice to you is to accept that and move on. After all you have many cherished moments with the one you loved......we all do....." again she became lost in thought. Concealing a breaking heart that she would never reveal to the others. A Queen would do no such thing.

India felt it her duty to comfort mother with the loss but really they were comforting each other. As the days went on all of them, cats and people alike, healed the wounds left behind when death comes to your door.

There they stood, Robbie, the Scaredy Cat, India despised him. She ridiculed his shyness and felt him weak. She adored Miss Davis, after all, she was the baby. Paige was still an outsider, not one of the original group. All kept a respectable distance from India. Even when Mother and Dad saw it fit to bring a puppy home, it too learned what respect was.

India spent her nights cuddling with Mother and Dad, well why not? She had been doing so for a dozen years. If anyone else tried to move in on her territory then claws would certainly be bared and so would teeth. Paige, Robbie and Rozie the dog thought it best to steer clear of the Queen. Bette, however, was in awe of her majesty and never strayed too far from her. She was both quite often impressed and perplexed by India and yet she found her interesting enough to idolize. India didn't seem to notice the complimentary shadow.

No one, certainly not India would ever expect her accepting the royal crown that she would ever have to defend it or Prince Street itself but that is exactly what happened. It was July when a rat found it's way into the house through the cellar. His filthy coat and rotted teeth were disgusting to the well pampered animals that resided at Prince Street. Rats are selfish animals and he was no exception. Rozie, the dog, was first to discover the intruder. She confronted him, barking. Feeling trapped and cornered, the dirty rodent attacked the innocent pup. In a flash India appeared from no where and savagely attacked the menace almost ripping him to shreds.

Terrified, Rozie ran to her bed and buried her head. India put the best pounding on the rodent that she could and immediately tossed him down the stairs and out the door into the street where he belonged. Tattered and bleeding she immediately ran a hot bath and immersed herself into a foamy anti-bacterial bath and cleansed her wounds as best she could.

This could be a very dangerous event as India, at her age and with the feline-leukemia virus in her system, might very well have spelled the end for her. However, doing things her way, she was able to bounce back. Bette, Paige and Robbie were none the wiser, all peacefully sleeping in their clean and comfortable spots. Rozie, shaken and scared, was thankful for all that India was able to do to fend off the intruding enemy. Still a relative newcomer to their home, she knew India was so much more than she seemed. She realized the truth about who and why India was the reserved and stand-offish feline that she appeared to be. A maverick, a leader and a heroine, India vonhalkien, Queen of the Castle. For years she would reign with a tight fist and an even tighter attitude. Paige would often refer to her as the Ice Queen.

The average life expectancy for a cat is 8-9 years anything beyond that is credited to the care-givers, the quality of food and the perseverance of the feline themselves. When a cat like India reaches the age of fourteen she has pretty much accomplished more than most. Outlasting all predictions of her demise, she fought the feline leukemia virus for nearly eleven years. This summer it got the best of her. She first started to show signs of decline with a loss of appetite. Daddy was the one who noticed first. He would spoil her with cooked salmon, liver and chicken, all the things she loved. He would spend enormous amounts of time with her and making sure she was comfortable. But after a while the appetite was not there. She was becoming weak and so to ensure her safety from falling and getting seriously hurt, Mother and Daddy gave up their bed. Here she was convalescing comfortably with Daddy often lying by her side, talking and singing to her. Despite her weakening state she still found her way to him as though he was the one needing comforting.

In her eyes he was able to see that look that left him crying in his heart. He took the time to tell her how much he loved her and how much having her in his life made him feel so much more important than before she had ever come along. He told her long ago that he would take care of her until the day she died and he held true to his promise.

As the summer days dwindled India found the light breeze that blew in the bedroom window relaxing on her aging body and Daddy's company even more so. In the evenings she had full view of the night sky and the moon hung full and bright. It was beautiful. Her thoughts were drifting back through the years and there was Rory and Angel and Daddy and Mother and Daddy again. He was always there. Near dawn, India thought she heard a rustling in the tree outside the window but realized that maybe it was just the wind.

In a rare turn of events Paige, who never showed any interest in the outside world, ran away from home. After searching for days, Daddy found her and she was returned safely to her home. So out of character, she simply explained that she had a mission to accomplish and she did just that. That seemed to be the end of that. Paige has never been one to offer any explanations to anyone.

The bedroom door was closed most of the time and no one was allowed to bother India her delicate state. Paige refused to show any concern, Robbie watched from afar, but Bette lingered near the room always within arm's length of the one she held in such high regard. "Take care of your father for me" she whispered to the little one. Bette began to weep.

Only once Robbie appeared at the foot of the bed. India motioned for him to come closer. She began to softly speak "I know it seemed that I never loved you but I want you to know that I care for you deeply. I snarled at your weakness, I scoffed at your nervousness and I cajoled your sensitive personality in hopes that it might make you stronger. You will, after all, soon be crowned the new King of Prince Street." Robbie shivered at the thought. "I'm not worthy, I never was. I was sickly as a boy and weak as a man and I am not ready for the responsibility of such a great title"

India, barely able to move on her own, lay swaddled and weak. "The responsibility is yours whether you like it or not. Always remember, put Prince Street and it's residents first and your own needs second and you will be okay, I am proud of you". With that remark his heart became flooded with emotion. He walked away prouder that moment that any other in his life. He knew where his responsibilities lay and accepted his fate.

In was in the morning when India took her last breath. Daddy was right there where he always was and her last moments were with him. At the precise instant she died, Daddy felt a deep spiritual connection to his baby and to the almighty. Paige and Robbie sat motionless upon hearing the news and neither spoke. Bette cried softly and was comforted by Rozie who whispered to her "she was a brave and mighty woman who fought for each and every one of us. Come with me and I will tell you about last summer...and a dirty rat."

A sombre cloud engulfed Prince Street and although all knew it was coming it didn't make it any easier. Daddy knew what had to be done and did so. Bette and Rozie talked about India and the rat incident. Robbie stared silently out the window anticipating the future. Paige showed no emotion on her face and returned to her bed. As she made herself comfortable, a single tear dropped from her eye onto the silk cushion that was her bed. A far cry, she thought to herself, from crouching near the woodpile to shut out the driving rain.

But it was another teardrop that fell that meant so much more. From high in the tree teardrops softly fell from the eyes of a grateful raccoon who had lingered outside Prince Street bedroom window for days and would lovingly gaze upon the soft sleeping face of someone he truly loved. He was grateful to Paige for informing him.

God Bless and keep India, and all the cat babies and all babies out there. It's cruel world you know but a cuddle certainly make a huge difference. After all isn't love what we live to know?

PS   A note from Daddy.   Fourteen years is a long time to get to know someone and to share a life. India, the feisty broad was used to doing things her way and in death was no exception. No trips to the vet, no complaining, no fuss, she simply took over Daddy's bed and it was there she said goodbye. I spent the last few days with her and I rarely left her side. Despite her ill health she snuggled and seemed to comfort me like she knew what was coming. In my heart I cried because I was losing my closest companion but on the other hand I continued to marvel at her strength and determination.

Between two trees in our backyard I laid my girl to rest. No fuss, no funeral, just her, just me. I had promised her when I brought her home that I would take care of her until the day she died, and I did. She in return, accepted me as her one and only. A true honour! So onward I march as she would expect me to but every once in a while, I cannot help but look over my shoulder and remember how her loving me made me feel.

Goodbye my love, I have no intention of ever letting your memory escape the interior of my heart nor the walls of my very soul. I honestly love You.

Let's end all of this on a happy note...read on and thanks for taking the time to visit.

A Prince Street Christmas

The door to the living room was closed. Mother had been in there all day and Bette was curious as to what she was up to. It was difficult for her to see underneath the door and all she could hear was the emptying of boxes and the rattling of paper. Bette was determined to get to the bottom of this mystery but unfortunately she fell asleep waiting. "Oh my little baby" said Mommy. Bette opened her sleepy eyes and looked up at her mother. She was very tired and for a moment forgot all about the mystery in the living room. But then all at once she was able to see it for herself. It was the most beautiful sight Bette had ever seen. A cat's dream comes true, a decorated Christmas tree complete with garland and bulbs and even little birds in nests and a star to top it all off.

Immediately she walked over to it and under it and around it. Bette was so excited that there really was nothing else that she could do but climb it so up the middle she went. It was a pine tree so it smelled wonderful and with all the lights and tinsel and other decorations, Bette knew that it must have been put there in the living room just for her. But Mother felt differently.

All Mother's hard work could not have been in vain. She reached her hand into the middle of the tree and scooped Bette out. Out into the hall she marched and Bette was placed on the floor in front of her. As Bette looked into Mother's face she kind of sensed that there was something wrong, but what could it be? Then Mother spoke. "Christmas trees are not for kittens!"

Imagine that! Bette thought to herself, Mother had to be kidding. After all trees are for climbing, birds are for catching and stars are for making wishes on. Therefore this is a tree, there are several birds in nests on the branches and that shiny star at the top must be for wishing upon, so that was that. It must have belonged to her.

Mother was determined to make Bette understand that this was to be considered another ornament, an untouchable one at that. "If you go near it again I will be forced to use the water bottle." Bette shivered at the mere mention of that. The water bottle meant business. Mother never has to resort to using such a cat hating weapon so she figured that this must be important. So Bette did had to admit one thing, that the tree should not be spoiled by anyone tampering with it. Still, in her eyes it certainly was a tempting thing of beauty.

Over on the chesterfield India was sleeping soundly rolled up in a ball. She too was excited about Christmas. To her it meant that both Mother and Dad would be home for a few days. India always enjoys that. Robbie was eyeing the gifts. He knows that with gifts come empty packages and those are fun to hide in. Rory although he is the mature one of the group still enjoys acting like a child all through the holidays. But the one thing to which they all can agree is that on Christmas Day there is certainly a reason to celebrate and that would be because of: the turkey dinner, and these cats like to eat!

By the time that Christmas Eve had rolled around the whole house was alive with holiday spirit. The music was light and bouncy, there was plenty of company and lots and lots to eat. Bette noticed that Mother and Dad were even taking an extra moment to sit and look at the tree and all the decorations. She knew that this time of year was special to them as well as to herself.

The evening was quiet. Mother and Dad had long since gone to slumber and India was comfortably sleeping at the end of their bed. Rory too was sound asleep in his bed on the trunk in the hall and Robbie (as usual) was in his safe place under the daybed in the den. But Bette was bright eyed on this particular night. She looked out the front window in the living room, up and down Prince Street. There wasn't a soul in sight. She assumed that everyone must be home in bed because there wasn't even any tire tracks in the snow. "Oh well" she thought. "I might as well settle down as well." She headed for the quilt on the love seat because it is so comfortable against a cat's skin. From where she was laying she could see the moon glistening in the cool night sky and watched as the snowflakes fell softly onto the lawn. She was content. Tomorrow is Christmas and we will all be together.

Now you have to remember a few things about Christmas and cats. It is not all fun and games. Frosted window panes are cold to the touch, candles can burn and why in the world would anybody want to roast chess nuts on an open fire?, and then eat them, they smell awful and they taste awful. But still it can be a happy time. Like when Santa came to visit. Bette was so happy to see him, although he wasn't like everybody else. His clothes were so bright and red and he had a long white beard. Daddy didn't look like that. But when he reached over to pat her on the head , Bette knew right away that there was something special about him. He was so kind and caring. Santa sat next to her on the love seat and was able to communicate with her in a way that humans cannot. He spoke without words to convey his message. He told Bette that she was lucky because she was one of the chosen ones. She was selected to come to Prince Street to add to the circle of love that existed there.

The funny thing was that Bette knew exactly what Santa was talking about. She was so grateful to get to know Mother and Dad and to become a part of such a family, especially since she had been so sick at birth. Bette almost died shortly after being born and she would have too had it not been for the kindness of Dr Gwen and her sister Juanita. It wasn't easy for them to give Bette up but they knew that if she went to Prince Street to live that it was going to be a long and healthy life. And it is.

He talked a little more about what her responsibility was to those who resided there with her at Prince Street. Bette's duty was to make sure that Mother is shown how much she is loved. Santa explained that the world needed more people like Mother. She is such a wonderful and beautiful person with a lot of love in her heart and she gives this love out to all those who need it in the quietest way possible and yet never asks for anything in return. Her reward is the love that she receives inside her home from her family of which you are a very special part. That to him was the real gift of Christmas, unconditional love for all living things.

And in a moment he was gone.

Bette had drifted off to sleep, but before long there was the rustle of paper and the opening of gifts. Bette was as excited as everyone else and she wasn't long delving into the middle of all of the excitement. She ran around in circles, thumped her brothers, played with her new cat toys and yet took the time to sit on Mother's lap and give her big loves. That is what makes Mother very happy and today of all days is no exception. Merry Christmas Mother!

From all of us at Prince Street to all of you out there we wish you warmth, love and all the best in this and every season.

Before we go I want to give you a glimpse into my next project FOOD for THOUGHT and introduce you to my "Dawg"

Little Boy Lost

When Christopher John Steel was born, I suspect he was like every other boy his age, his parent's pride and joy. There he was looking up into his mother's face, she, no doubt, was beaming with joy. At home, a sister who waited for her baby brother to arrive. Her mother told her at an early age to take her brother's hand and to look out for him. That is exactly what Elizabeth did then and tries to do today. Not that Christopher John Steel needs anyone to hold his hand as he is stubbornly determined, but it sure is nice to know someone loves you as much as Elizabeth does. And she does.

A father is always happy to have a son for many reasons, a smaller version of themselves, a chip off the old block and to carry on his name. The fact that this little brown eyed charmer was nearly born on his birthday, probably solidified their bond. Why wouldn't it?

But, as these things go, all may have looked perfect on the outside, there was trouble brewing beneath. All men, no matter who they are, carry demons and David was one who carried his fair share of those. While Alexis and Elizabeth surrounded the little boy and did their best to shield him from harm, still, the darkness took over. When David passed away, it left them all to say the least, broken. That brings me to today and to you because I, like you, was this little boy lost.

I know of what I speak, I was too young to lose a father. I did my best to keep all my feelings inside and to wear a brave face, but if the truth be known, my suffering ran deeper than even I ever realized. Still 30 years later, that man and his memory have never left me. I needed a father, I didn't have 'a' sister to take my hand, I had seven and a domineering mother to boot. I needed a man's touch and love and understanding. Even though my father had a large family, there was no one who could remotely fill the void. Despite the full and busy life I lead, I still carry with me, unanswered questions, insecurities that I mask with humour and sarcasm, and a real sense of being cheated by losing my father so young. What he didn't know was that he impacted my heart for a lifetime and left a rather significant imprint on my soul.

Thank GOD I had my mother! She took this nervous and insecure boy, stood him up, dusted him off and pushed him out the door everyday, assuring him he was going to be ok. And I am! I am quite a versatile person who never does anything half way. I intend to leave my mark on this earth one way or the other. I just wanted my mother to be proud of me, to have the respect of the young persons I come in contact with and to one day, over there, to embrace my father once more and to tell him how much I love him and how much I have thought about him over the years. Then I will know that my life is complete and that it meant something.

So, here we are today, I work as a teacher's assistant, among other things, and I am privy to all sorts of unique individuals and I must tell you, I've learned a lot. Not just life's lessons but things about myself that I was never fully able to explain. As a result of this internal investigation, I may have turned out OK. I work hard and I work lots. I am a productive person who is intent on being all I can be and getting the most out of my life. I married the only woman I will ever love, I live in a house that she turned into a home and all in all it is a pretty good life. I possess a gift of intuition that has helped me along the way. That intuition along with a heart that overflows with love for nature, the animal kingdom and the human beings I encounter, I am successful.

I believe that life is a gift, that friends and family add to all of this and it either makes you a better person or causes you to fall on your face. I have done both. I have however, emerged as a champion with a great ability to see beyond the face and into the soul. This happened the day I met you almost instantly. You stood heads above the crowd in your personality alone. You chose to down play your intelligence, you choose not to realize your potential but as these things go, you can no longer deny your abilities. You really are quite a guy. That is why Christopher John Steel, I expect no less of you in this life than your very best, to be all that you can be and to promise me that one day, when you have the blessing of looking down into a familiar pair of brown eyes, that you will do whatever you have to, to keep that little person safe, to set a proper example with a clear head, mind and heart and then I will know that I was right. You are OK.

God doesn't make mistakes and he sure didn't make one when he made you. If, in the unlikely event, that something happens to one of us, please know that this man, from where I am sitting, thinks an awful lot of you.

I love you boy!

Richard Todd Canton